John V. Hedtke

The

Awesome

Winning!

and Amazing

Insider's Book

of Windows Game

Tips,

Traps,

Peachpit Press

and Sneaky Tricks.

WINNING!
John V. Hedtke

PEACHPIT PRESS, INC.
2414 Sixth St.
Berkeley, CA 94710
(800) 283-9444
(510) 548-4393
(510) 548-5991 (fax)

ISBN 0-938151-77-0

0 9 8 7 6 5 4 3 2 1

Printed and bound in the United States of America

Dedicated to my Wife and Favorite Person,
Patricia Callander Hedtke,
who is herself Awesome and Amazing.

Only a book of this magnitude could be dedicated to her.

Acknowledgements

Many people have been important parts in creating this book. Every book is a collaboration of people and talents. A book's cover only lists the author and the publisher, but does not mention all the people who were vital to the book's creation. The following people have been of great assistance to the creation of *Winning!*, and deserve acknowledgment for their efforts:

First and foremost, I want to acknowledge Ann Miller and Kate Harper, without whose efforts this book would have been almost impossible. My deepest thanks to both of them. Next, Ted Nace, Publisher of Peachpit Press, for sharing my vision and publishing this book. Charles Fitzgerald, Microsoft Product Manager, and Lisa Forssell, Microsoft Program Manager, for their strong support and cooperation. Olav Martin Kvern, who once again plied his exceptional talents in creating the design for this book. Sally Fichet and John D. Berry, for clear vision, superior editing, and excellent advice. Byron Canfield, for fast and incredibly efficient production work. Patricia Hedtke and Helen Nace, whose combined creative talents produced the title for this book.

To the following people, who provided fascinating trivia about the games: Mike Blaylock (Pegged), Wes Cherry (Solitaire and Pipe Dream), Brad Christian (IdleWild), Michael F. C. Crick (WordZap), Robert Donner (Minesweeper and TicTactics), Dave Edson (TETRIS), Scott Ferguson (TetraVex), Chris Lee Fraley (RattlerRace and Rodent's Revenge), Robert Hogue (TriPeaks), Jim Horne (FreeCell and Life), Rick LaPlante (Tut's Tomb), Tito Messerli (JigSawed), Michael C. Miller (Stones), Henry Neils (Klotski), Dave Norris (Taipei), Chris Peters (Reversi), Chris Pirih (SkiFree), Ken Sykes (Cruel and Golf)

And to all the programmers of the Windows games, thanks for reminding everyone that computers are for more than just work.

Contents

Welcome!

Y ou're probably reading this because you know one of the Truths of the Universe: just because computers can help you write reports, balance your checkbook, and keep track of inventory doesn't mean that you can't have fun with them, too! This Basic Truth (along with about $39.95 list price) qualifies you to have fun playing the games in the Microsoft Entertainment Packs.

The Microsoft Entertainment Packs are collections of games, puzzles, and diversions that run under Microsoft Windows, including:

■ Cruel, Golf, FreeCell, Tut's Tomb, and TriPeaks, exciting and challenging solitaire card games.

■ TETRIS, a very popular game for years, and now available for Windows.

■ Pipe Dream, a colorful Windows version of the popular game from LucasFilms.

■ FujiGolf, an attractive video golf game set just outside of Mt. Fuji, Japan.

■ LifeGenesis, a Windows version of the popular Life computer game.

■ Klotski, a series of puzzles that can take from minutes to hours to solve.

■ IdleWild, a screen saver shipped with different sets of options in each volume of the Microsoft Entertainment Packs (collect the entire set!).

In addition, there are more than a dozen other Microsoft Entertainment Pack games, puzzles, and pastimes covered in this book.

The Microsoft Entertainment Packs are designed for the loosely supervised business person. (Please note that being at home counts as "loosely supervised," so it's okay to play these games on your home computer, too.) The idea behind all three volumes is that "Windows increases your productivity, but you don't need to give that productivity to your employer … keep it for yourself and play games with it!" Even some of the ads for the first Entertainment Pack had fine print at the bottom that said things like "If you're reading this, you have plenty of time to play games."

How Did We Get Here, Anyway?

When Microsoft Windows was first released, it just contained Reversi. Windows 2.0 still only contained Reversi, but programmers started experimenting with Windows to see what else they could whip up in the way of games (just as programming exercises, you understand). A number of

Who says you can't go home again? The release of the Microsoft Entertainment Pack marked Microsoft's re-entry into the retail game market. Although Microsoft had a number of popular games in its early days, most notably Adventure, it has not actively sold games for a number of years. Naysayers should note that Microsoft does not officially class Flight Simulator as a "game," but as a "simulation."

games started circulating unofficially within Microsoft. The release of Windows 3.0 saw the addition of a new game, Solitaire, which was an instant hit.

Shortly after Windows 3.0 came out, some of the games that had been underground hits inside Microsoft were polished, bundled, and sold as the Microsoft Entertainment Pack. Sales were really hot and the reviews were enthusiastic. Following the incredible success of this first Pack, two more game packs were released in the fall of 1991: the Microsoft Entertainment Packs, Volumes Two and Three.

The rest of this chapter tells you what equipment you need to run the Microsoft Entertainment Packs, how to install them on your computer, and general information about using a mouse and game commands.

What Equipment Do You Need?

To run the Microsoft Entertainment Packs, you need a computer with a mouse. You also need Microsoft Windows version 3.0 or greater. The mouse is essential—although Windows is technically usable without a mouse, it's not particularly convenient. More importantly, many games in the Microsoft Entertainment Packs require a mouse.

Unlike some Windows applications, the Microsoft Entertainment Packs don't require super fast computers with lots of memory. You can run all the games on a garden-variety 286 with 1 megabyte of memory and a 40-megabyte hard disk if you like.

Monitors. You need an EGA monitor and card, at the very least. A VGA or Super VGA monitor and card are better. Some special effects in the games don't work without a VGA monitor. If you don't have a VGA and you decide to shop for one, remember that they're not all created equal. In general, the smaller the dot pitch (the size of the dot on the screen), the better the picture looks. There are monochrome (black and white) VGA monitors, but if you're playing games, after all, you ought to go for color.

As a matter of fact, you can use your favorite Windows game to see what each monitor looks like. Take a write-protected backup copy of your game diskette to the store, run the game from the diskette, and compare the color and resolution. Then buy the monitor that makes you happiest without mortally wounding your finances for the month.

Mouse or Keyboard?

You're going to have to use a mouse with most of the games. Many games have only minimal keyboard support. Indeed, some (such as Tut's Tomb), cannot be played with the keyboard at all. On the other hand, a few games (like TETRIS) are much easier with the keyboard, and at least one game (SkiFree) has many options available on the keyboard that aren't available at all with a mouse. Most shortcuts and sneaky tricks are done from the keyboard using a combination of keys.

Installing the Microsoft Entertainment Packs

Installing the Microsoft Entertainment Packs is very simple. In fact, you can use the same installation procedure for all three volumes:

1. Insert the Microsoft Entertainment Pack diskette in your computer. If you're using 3.5" disks, you may have two diskettes. If so, insert the first diskette in your computer.
2. Start Microsoft Windows.
3. Choose Run from the File menu. The Run dialog box appears.
4. Type A:\SETUP and press Enter. This runs the setup program on the diskette in the A: drive. (If you're installing from the B: drive, type B:\SETUP and press Enter). The setup procedure starts. After a moment, you're prompted for the directory to install the Microsoft Entertainment Pack files into.

5. Either press Enter to accept the default directory (C:\WEP) or type a new drive and directory and press Enter. The setup program copies the files from the diskette to your hard drive. This process takes a few minutes. If you're installing from two 3.5" disks, the setup program prompts you when you need to switch diskettes.

6. As the final step in the setup procedure, the setup program creates a program group window for the games and adds the icons for each game to the window. The program groups for the three volumes are named (unsurprisingly) Entertainment Pack, Entertainment Pack Two, and Entertainment Pack Three. That's it! You're ready to play games now.

Installing Several Entertainment Packs

If you're installing several Entertainment Packs at once, you should install the Entertainment Packs in the same directory on your hard disk (usually C:\WEP). Also, if you're installing Microsoft Entertainment Pack: Volume One and either Volumes Two or Three, install Volume One first. Doing these things makes sure that you'll be using the latest version of the IdleWild screen saver program. More importantly, because there are different IdleWild modules in each Entertainment Pack, installing everything in one directory lets you use all the modules regardless of which program group you start IdleWild from.

Using a Mouse for the First Time

Using a mouse is very easy, but if you've never used a mouse before, there are a few basic concepts you need to know.

The mouse *pointer* is usually an arrow, but can be other things as well. For example, the mouse pointer in Klotski is a little hand. In Pipe Dream it's a tiny pipe wrench!

Pointing is moving the mouse pointer so that it is directly over some object.

Clicking is lightly pressing the left mouse button once.

Double-clicking is clicking the left mouse button twice quickly. Double-clicking a game icon starts the game. Double-clicking objects within a game may also have other effects, such as moving cards to the suit stacks in Solitaire.

Dragging is holding the left mouse button down while moving the mouse. The object the mouse is pointing to moves along with the mouse pointer. When the object is where you want it, let go of the left mouse button.

All these mouse instructions are for right-handed mouse operation. If you're left-handed, you can use the Control Panel in Microsoft Windows to reset the mouse for left-handed operation. See the *Microsoft Windows User's Guide* for information about how to do this.

Game Commands

You can start, exit, set options in, and get Help in all the games by using a mouse to choose options from the menu bar at the top of each game window. You can also use your keyboard to choose game commands.

All programs designed for use with Microsoft Windows let you pull down menus by holding down the Alt key and pressing the underlined character in the menu name. For example, to pull down a Game menu, the key combination is Alt-G. To pull down an Options menu, press Alt-O. Two alternate ways to execute a command on the pulled-down menu are to type the underlined character in that command *or* highlight the command with the arrow keys and press Enter.

In addition to the standard Windows keyboard interface, most of the games have shortcut keys. Help on rules of the game, how to play, commands, and options is available by pressing F1. Pressing F2 starts a new game for most of the games (Solitaire and Reversi, which came with your version of Windows, are exceptions). You can pause some games by pressing F3. (This feature appears on timed or action games, such as Tetris and Pipe Dream.) Pressing F3 again restarts the game, as does pressing any key on the keyboard or clicking the mouse.

Some of the games have an "undo" feature. If you change your mind about the move you just made, press Backspace to take back the move. But beware: some games penalize you in time or points for undoing a move.

One very important key is the panic button, also known as the "boss" key. If your boss walks by, pressing Esc minimizes the game screen instantly, letting you look as if you're actually busy with something the boss intends to pay you for. Try the panic button a couple of times before it becomes a hot issue for your continued employment; not all games have this feature. You should also be aware that the endgame sequence in some games takes a long time to display, during which time pressing Esc won't work immediately. Be ready to hit the big, red "Game Over" switch if your boss walks by right then.

To exit a game completely, open the Game menu by pressing Alt-G, then press X (for Exit). Exiting keeps your score from being tallied in some games (which could be a good thing if you're not playing up to snuff that day). Another way to shut down a game is to double-click on the top-left button of the game window.

Many of the games also share a way to cheat! Ctrl-Shift-F10 on many games in Volumes Two and Three frequently shows you the endgame sequence. This feature was added for the testers so they could check out the winning game scenarios without having to spend hours playing and winning the game to test each possible configuration.

Remember: a given game may not have every one of these features, so try each game out and see what's there. Special features peculiar to one or two games are discussed in the individual chapters.

Using this Book

The rest of this book is divided into four sections. The first section, Games with Windows, describes the two games included with Windows 3.0, Solitaire and Reversi. The remaining sections tell you how to play the games in each of the three volumes of the Microsoft Entertainment Packs.

Each chapter in a section describes a single game. The chapters start with information about the object of the game, the playing area, and game pieces. After this, you get to see how to play the game and learn about winning strategies (the keyboard shortcuts appear in a sidebar in this part). Last is a section of tips, traps, and sneaky tricks (the good part): all the things that will make you a whiz at the game and put you miles ahead of your friends.

Where to buy 'em

Can't find the Microsoft Entertainment Packs locally? Microsoft does not handle any direct sales of the Microsoft Entertainment Packs, but you can call 1-800-426-9400 for the name of the nearest dealer or for more information.

Part 1

Games with Windows

The first section covers the two games that are shipped with Microsoft Windows:

CHAPTER 1

Solitaire

There are hundreds of versions of Solitaire, several of which are included in the Windows Entertainment Packs. The version that comes with Microsoft Windows is actually called Klondike, or Canfield. It's not the quickest form of Solitaire, nor the easiest, and winning it depends almost completely on luck. Despite these shortcomings, Klondike has been the most popular single-player card game for decades.

Wes Cherry came up with Solitaire several years ago, as a programming exercise to teach himself Windows. Judging by the product, he learned pretty darned well.

Object of the Game

From the initial layout (the *tableau*) and the draw pile (called the *stock*), you have to build complete thirteen-card sequences (runs) in each suit from ace to king. You win if you can move all the cards in the tableau and the stock to the four suit stacks.

Game Window

The four suit stacks are shaded outlines in the top-right corner of the window. They're empty at the beginning of the game. The stacks of cards that form the tableau are in a row across the middle of the window. At the beginning of the game, there are seven stacks of cards in the tableau,

Basic Solitaire layout

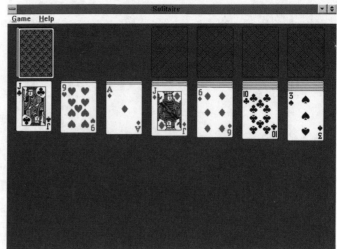

each with one to seven cards as you move from left to right. The top card of each stack is face up; the rest are hidden.

The stock is in the top-left corner. There's a blank space beside it for the cards you turn over. The score and the elapsed time appear at the bottom of the window.

Below the title bar are the Game and Help menus, which let you start a new game, set options, and bring up the Help screens if you need them.

Play!

Starting the game. Start the game by clicking on the Solitaire icon in the Games group window. Solitaire automatically deals a hand for you, using the last options you set or the default options if you're running Solitaire for the first time. (More on setting options later; sit back and enjoy the game for now.) You can play the hand you were dealt or deal a new one by choosing Deal from the Game menu.

Moves. Solitaire gives you three basic kinds of moves.

Create runs in the tableau. First, try to rearrange the cards in the tableau to create runs and uncover hidden cards. Move a card from one place to another by dragging it.

*Rearranging cards before
drawing from the stock*

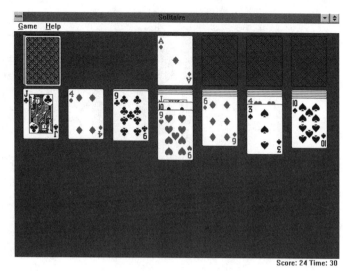

You build up runs in the tableau in descending sequence and alternating colors (or light and dark suits if you're using a monochrome monitor). For example, a red queen goes on a black king, a black jack on a red queen, and so on. If you try to make an illegal move, such as a black ten on a black jack, the card drifts back to its position when you let go of the mouse button.

You can pick up a whole run of cards by dragging the highest card in the sequence you want to move. All cards below this card in the column move along with it. You can also move just part of a run if you want to.

After you move all the face-up cards from one stack to another in the tableau, turn over the top face-down card on the stack. When you've turned over all the cards in a stack, you're left with an open space. You can fill an open space only with a run that starts with a king or with a king by itself, either from another stack in the tableau or from the stock, which we talk about later.

Build runs on your aces. The second kind of move in this version of Solitaire lets you start the suit stack runs. Unlike the tableau run, a suit stack run starts with an ace and builds in ascending order in the same suit.

Draw from the stock

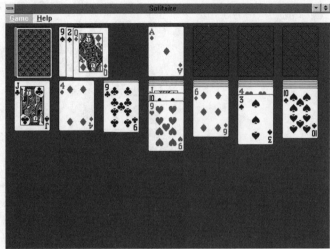

Score: 16 Time: 76

If you uncover an ace, play it on one of the four suit stacks at the top of the screen. If you like, you can just double-click on the card; the computer moves it up to the top of the screen. As you uncover more cards for the suit stacks (ace, two, three, and so on), double-click on those to send them quickly to the right stack. Double-click rather than drag to speed up your game and win with monster points! Be sure to double-click on the center of the cards.

Draw from the stock. When you run out of tableau possibilities and you can't do anything with the suit stacks, your third move is to turn cards from the stock, to try to complete the tableau runs. You draw cards from the stock either one or three at a time (typically three), depending on the Draw option you've chosen. To draw cards, click on the stock. The cards appear face up to the right of the stock.

You can only play the top card of the draw at any time. Once you've played it, you can play the next card down, and so on. Click on the stock for more cards. When you run out of cards in the stock, you'll see a green "O." Click on the "O" to turn the stock over and go through it again.

Playing Vegas style. You're probably most familiar with the standard version of Solitaire. With a little practice, you should be able to win fairly often. If so, you'll like Vegas-style Solitaire, which is much harder and has stricter rules.

To play Solitaire with Vegas rules, choose Vegas Scoring from the Game Options menu. Although the Vegas layout looks the same as the standard game, the Vegas game limits the number of times you can run through the stock. When you go through the stock the last time, you see a red "X" instead of a green "O" on the empty stock pile. The "X" means that you can't go through the stock again: once you finish moving the cards on the tableau, the game's over. You can go through the stock either once or three times, depending on whether you pick Draw One or Draw Three on the Game Options menu.

Setting options. Pick different game options from the Game Options menu. You can specify either one or three cards turned over at a time from the stock by choosing Draw One or Draw Three.

The Timed game option shows the elapsed time for each game at the bottom of the screen.

From the keyboard

To move a card, position the pointer with the left and right arrow keys, then press Enter or the spacebar. The card lifts slightly (or the outline appears, if Outline Dragging is turned on). Use the left and right arrow keys to move the card to its new location, then press Enter or the spacebar to release it.

To move a stack of cards, put the pointer on the stack, then use the up and down arrow keys to move the pointer to the highest card you want to move in the stack.

To turn a card over, put the pointer on the card and press Enter.

You cannot press F1 for Help or F2 to start a new game.

The Status bar option gives you status information at the bottom of the Solitaire window.

When you choose Outline Dragging, Solitaire shows an outline of the card when you move it. If the outline passes over a space or card on which you can play the card you're moving, the space or card changes color.

Standard scoring lets you turn the stock over as many times as you want and scores using standard rules. Vegas scoring limits the number of times you can turn the stock over and scores using Vegas rules (it takes your money).

If you change the Timed game, Draw, or Scoring options during a game, Solitaire deals a new hand.

Dealer! Fresh deck please!

You can change the card backs to match your mood. When you choose the Game Deck option, Solitaire displays a dozen card-back designs. (A good color VGA monitor is important here.) Click on the design you want, then click on OK. Solitaire changes the card backs to your choice (but it doesn't redeal the cards, as it does when you change the scoring options).

Most of the designs (artfully executed by Leslie Kooy) are what they seem, but four are animated when you display them on a VGA monitor. The robot's meter moves while its lights blink green and red. The bats around the castle fly (look closely; you'll see the little wings flapping away). The hand holding the cards is called "Slime" and was inspired by a Grateful Dead song "Doing That Rag" that mentions "Aces running up and down your sleeve;" every 15 seconds, the fourth ace pops up from the sleeve.

The card back with palm trees is called "San Felipe." Wes came up with the card to remind him of time he spent there on spring breaks from Harvey Mudd. Every 50 seconds, the sun does one of three things (watch carefully; it only takes about a second): puts on sunglasses; puts on sunglasses and smiles; puts on sunglasses, smiles, and sticks its tongue out at you.

Endgame. You win when all the cards in the deck are on the suit stacks. Winning starts a wonderful animation of bouncing, cascading cards—it's well worth the effort. You can interrupt this if you want by pressing any key or clicking the mouse. Start a new game by clicking on Yes in the "Deal Again?" dialog box that appears. Choose No if you want to set other options before starting a new game.

More often, you'll probably lose. You'll know—there won't be any more moves to make. To try Solitaire again, click on Deal in the Game menu.

To quit the game, choose Exit from the Game menu. Quitting Windows automatically quits the game, and also wipes out your score.

Scoring and Winning

In Standard scoring, you earn 10 points for moving a card to the suit stacks and 5 points for moving a card from the stock to the tableau. You lose 15 points for moving a card from the suit stacks to the tableau. You also lose 20 points for turning the deck over more than three times when you're playing Draw Three, or 100 points when you're playing Draw One. If you're playing a timed game in Standard scoring, you can earn extra points for playing fast.

In Vegas scoring, you start by paying $52 for the deck. You then earn $5 for each card you move to the suit stacks. You need to play 11 cards to the suit stacks to break even. Choose the Keep Score option to balance your winnings and losses from game to game. There's no bonus for fast play in Vegas scoring, so take your time.

You can also say "The heck with it" and turn scoring off altogether by picking None from the Game Options menu.

Tips, Traps, and Sneaky Tricks

Though this version of Solitaire's based largely on luck, certain strategies can give you an edge. For instance, you should try to reduce the largest stack of cards in the tableau first, particularly if there's a choice between two cards. If

Card-game vocabulary, or, say that slowly, pardner

Ace The lowest-ranked card in a *suit*, with a value of 1.

Back up [v.] To take back the last card you played, or undo your last move, usually by clicking Undo or Back up on the Game menu or pressing the Backspace key. See also *Undo*.

Column A vertical layout of cards, displayed face up and overlapping so that the *rank* and *suit* of each card are visible. The bottom card in the column is exposed and is usually playable. A column of face-up cards may conceal a *stack* of face-down cards, as in Solitaire.

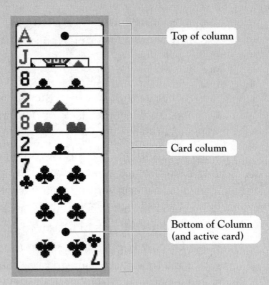

Top of column

Card column

Bottom of Column (and active card)

Deuce The second-ranked card in a *suit*, with a value of 2.

Discard pile A pile of cards that have been discarded from the game, or that have been dealt but can't be played.

Rank The value of each card, in order. The ace is the lowest-ranked card, then the deuce, then the three, and so on. After ten comes the jack, then the queen, then the king. The king is the highest-ranked card in most card games. (In some games, such as poker, the ace has the highest rank, and the lowest-ranked card is the deuce.)

Run A sequence of cards in order, such as deuce, three, four, five, six. The nature of a run varies from game to game. A run may be a sequence in the same *suit*, or alternating black and red *suits*, or all *suits*. A run may be in ascending order or descending order, depending on the game.

Stack A pile of cards in the *tableau*. A stack exposes only the top card. Cards in a stack may be face up, face down, or all but the top card face down (as in Solitaire).

Stock The pile of cards, face down, that haven't been dealt or played yet. You draw cards from the *stock*.

Suit One of the four families of cards: hearts, clubs, diamonds, and spades. Each *suit* contains a complete *run* of cards from ace to king.

Suit stack A *stack* on which you put only cards of the same suit. It may be face up or face down, depending on the game.

Tableau The layout of the cards in the play area. For the purposes of this book, the tableau generally doesn't include suit stacks, the stock, or the discard pile.

Undo Undo your last move, usually by clicking Undo or Back up on the Game menu or pressing the Backspace key. See also *Back up*.

there's a choice between using a card from the tableau and using one from the stock, take the card from the tableau. If you set the options to Draw Three, playing a single card from the stock near the beginning of a pass through the stock changes the cards that appear on the next pass.

If you need to, you can play cards off the suit stacks. You might want to do this so you can play the top card from the stock and then use the next card down or change the sequence of cards in the stock on the next pass. This can sometimes give you the edge you need to win a game (although it costs points off your score).

Almost everyone cheats at Solitaire occasionally. Here are some ways you can do it on the computer.(Readers of high moral fiber who would *never* stoop to cheating at Solitaire should skip the rest of this chapter.) If you're playing the Draw Three option but you just can't get to that one card in the middle of a group that you need, hold down Ctrl-Alt-Shift and click on the undealt stock. One card appears, just as if you were using the Draw One option. When you release Ctrl-Alt-Shift, Solitaire deals the cards from the stock in threes as usual. Using this sneaky trick doesn't trigger a redeal, nor does it appear on the score.

You can build up truly massive points by printing some colossal file as an Encapsulated PostScript file, then starting Solitaire. (See the manuals with your Microsoft Windows applications for information on how to print a PostScript file to the hard disk.) What happens is that all the activity of printing the file to the disk slows down the amount of time that Windows can pay attention to Solitaire, the clock gets confused, and you have more actual time to play than the clock accounts for. Since the bonus for winning a game is directly related to how fast you finished, the result is a record-breaking time and score. (Sorry, this trick requires Windows to do two things at once, so it only works on 386 computers or better.)

I *knew* you wanted to know how to cheat at Solitaire.

Reversi

 eversi has been around for a long time. If you've ever played Gabriel Industries' reversible disk game, Othello, you have some notion how Reversi works. Before Othello, people played reversible disk games with checkers on a checkerboard. One player played with the crown-side up and the other with the crown-side down. It's all the same game.

Reversi as a computer game was one of the original programs written for Windows and shipped with the first version of the program. Chris Peters of Microsoft wrote it.

Object of the Game

In Reversi, your opponent is the computer. Both you and the computer have a supply of reversible disks (thus, Reversi)—red on one side, blue on the other. You play red. (If you have a monochrome monitor, you play the white disks and the computer plays the black.) The object of Reversi is to finish the game with red disks dominating an eight-by-eight-square grid. You accomplish this by outflanking and capturing your opponent's disks. If you succeed, the disk flips to its red side—it's now yours.

Game Window

The opening Reversi window consists of a grid with sixty-four squares, eight to a side. Two red disks and two blue disks cover the four center squares.

Starting screen for Reversi

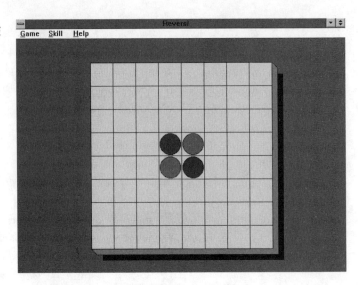

Reversi gives you three menus: Game, Skill, and Help. Use the Skill menu to choose one of the four skill levels: Beginner, Novice, Expert, or Master. A checkmark appears by the active skill level.

Play!

Starting the game. Double-click on the Reversi icon in the Games group window. The game's ready to play as soon as the window appears.

Moves. In Reversi, you have the (dubious) advantage of the opening move. But you can force the computer to take the opening move by choosing Pass from the Game menu.

Reversi has only one kind of move: you and the computer take turns putting one disk on any legal square. To place a disk, move the pointer to a square and click (the pointer changes from an arrow to a cross when it's on a legal square). If you try to put a disk on an illegal square, the computer says "You may only move to a space where the cursor is a cross. Click OK to continue." Be careful where you move; Reversi doesn't let you undo or back up.

Here's the definition of a legal square: any square that's right next to a blue disk (your opponent's disk) and in a direct line with a red disk on the other side of the blue disk. (There may be any number of blue disks in a line between the red disks.) The line can be in any direction—horizontal, vertical, or diagonal.

All the blue disks you can outflank with your red ones flip to their red side and become your property. A move can outflank any number of rows, in any number of directions at the same time.

If you can't make a legal move, the computer says "You must Pass" in the title bar. To pass, choose Pass from the Game menu. If you have a legal move, you can't opt to pass (except on the first move of the game). If the computer can't make a legal move, it displays the word Pass in the title bar. You get to take that turn.

Skill levels. The computer plays at the skill level you choose, spending more time to calculate its moves at the higher levels. Reversi defaults to the Beginner skill level— the computer looks only one move ahead.

To change to another skill level, choose Novice, Expert, or Master from the Skill menu. Novice looks three moves ahead. The machine studies all its own possible moves, as well as all your possible replies. Then it examines all of its own next possible moves.

At the Expert level, the machine looks five moves ahead: computer moves, your replies, computer moves,

From the keyboard

To play Reversi directly from the keyboard, use the arrow keys to position the pointer. (The pointer changes from an arrow to a cross when you're on a square that gives you a legal move.) Then press the spacebar or Enter to place your red disk. To shrink the game window to an icon, press Esc.

your replies, and computer moves. At the Master level you're forced to wait while the computer looks seven moves ahead. This can be a painfully slow process—especially if you've got a 286 machine—so you might want to run out for a six-pack while the computer figures out what it's going to do next.

Endgame. The game is over when neither you nor the computer has any legal moves left. You win if the red disks outnumber the blue disks. You lose if there are more blue disks than red.

    You can start a new game any time by choosing New from the Game menu. To quit Reversi, double-click on the top-left button of the Reversi window.

Scoring and Winning

When you win (which you won't for hours), the computer says "You Won by x," where x is the number of red disks less blue disks at the end of the game. When you lose, the computer says "You Lost by y," where y is the number of blue disks less red at the end of the game.

Tips, Traps, and Sneaky Tricks

Reversi can give you a hint for a legal move at any point during the game. From the Game menu, choose Hint. A cross appears briefly on the square the computer suggests. If you want to put your disk there, click the square. If not, move to another legal square and click. If you ask for another hint without making a move, the computer simply repeats its first suggestion; it doesn't suggest an alternative.

    Reversi is always predictable, but it isn't always the best advisor. If you play the computer's hints all the way through a game, Reversi always responds the same way. By taking the advice offered, you win at the Beginner level by four points, but at the Novice level you lose by twenty. At the Expert level you win by twelve, and lose by four at the Master level.

The first bit of advice you'll get from any experienced Reversi or Othello player is not to start out trying to flip the most disks at each turn. If you do, you're going to lose. In fact, you want to take exactly the opposite strategy at the beginning of the game: try to make moves that force your opponent to flip the most number of disks. That leaves you with the maximum possible flips later.

The computer tries to take certain squares and to prevent you from taking them. You should play the same way. Start by trying to place the red disks in the sixteen squares at the center of the board—the "sweet sixteen." Do this until all these squares are occupied. If at all possible, avoid moving into the corner squares just outside the sixteen center squares. These put you in the most vulnerable position to be outflanked by the computer. You'll also want to try and avoid any square between the sixteen center squares and the outside squares. Using them may give the computer easy access to an outside square.

Corners—try to take these.

Avoid these squares immediately adjacent to the corners.

Take the sides, if you can.

Avoid these squares.

The "sweet sixteen"

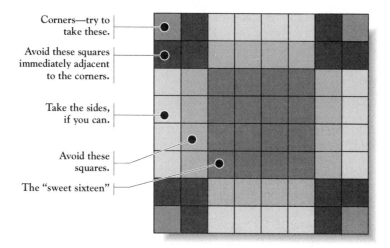

The corners of the board are extremely valuable—they can't be outflanked and they anchor three directions. If the computer does take a corner, you can reduce the strength of that position by capturing the square next to it. However, never place your piece on a square right next to an *empty* corner; that gives the computer too much advantage.

Taking three or four corners puts you in an excellent position to win. If you take two and the computer takes two, you've got a fight on your hands. If you're playing on a real board against a human opponent and only get one corner or none at all, the only sensible thing to do is have a coughing fit and upset the board. If you find yourself in that predicament while playing the computer, promise yourself you'll be more careful next time and start a new game.

Outside squares are almost as valuable as corners. They can be outflanked in only two directions but can serve as the anchoring end for five directions.

Easier ain't always. …If you play at the Beginner level, you may have more trouble following the action, because the computer plays so quickly you can't see what's happening. A lot of players actually win more games at the higher skill levels because the computer takes more time to move, making it possible for you to track what it's doing.

It's only a matter of time

Because Reversi may take quite a while to make its move or suggest a hint, you may want to disable Blank Pointer on the Options menu in IdleWild, if you're running IdleWild as a screen saver. This prevents the hourglass from disappearing, and you aren't left wondering what's happening. See page 43 for help with IdleWild's Blank Pointer option.

Part 2

The Microsoft Entertainment Pack: Volume One

The Microsoft Entertainment Pack: Volume One first appeared in 1990. It includes the following eight games:

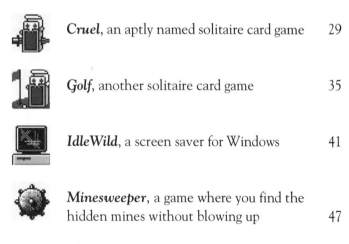

more...   ⬇

CHAPTER 3

Cruel

lthough Solitaire is the most popular of the one-player card games, a lot of other fascinating and frustrating single-player card games exist. One of the most intriguing is Cruel, written by Ken Sykes. Ken wrote the computer version of Cruel because he liked playing it but got tired of shuffling and dealing by hand.

Object of the Game

The idea in Cruel is to build thirteen-card runs from ace to king in each suit on the suit stacks at the top of the window. You win by moving all the cards from the tableau to the four suit stacks. (For definitions of card game terms, see the chapter on Solitaire, page 18.)

Game Window

The game starts with the four aces arranged at the top of the window. These are the bases of the suit stacks. Cruel also lays out a tableau of the remaining forty-eight cards in two rows of six stacks each. Each stack contains four cards, face up. Unlike Solitaire, Cruel doesn't give you a stock of spare cards; all the cards are laid out in the tableau and on the suit stacks at the start of the game. A Deal button, used to redeal the cards, is to the right of the suit stacks.

The three menus at the top of the game window let you start a new game, look at past scores, quit the game, turn

Basic Cruel layout
(to a heart that's tru-ue)

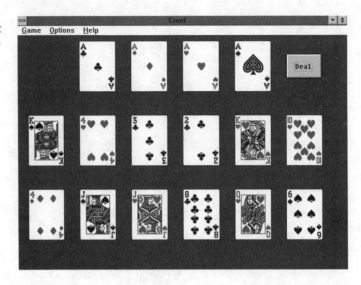

messages on or off, and choose a new deck of cards. To see the Help windows, click on the Help menu bar or press F1.

Play!

Starting the game. Click on the Cruel icon in the Entertainment Pack group window. Windows loads Cruel, ready to play the first game.

Moves. The idea here is to rearrange the cards in the tableau until you can stack them all in ascending rank by suit in the suit stacks. You can move cards from the tableau to the suit stacks or among stacks in the tableau.

From the tableau to the suit stacks. You can move a card to a suit stack if the card is in the same suit as the last card on the suit stack and one rank higher. For example,

---

From the keyboard

Cruel gives you only a few keyboard options. To start a new game, press F2. To get help, press F1. To back up a move, press Backspace. To shrink the game window to an icon, press Esc.

You can't move cards with the keyboard.

At least three moves are possible here

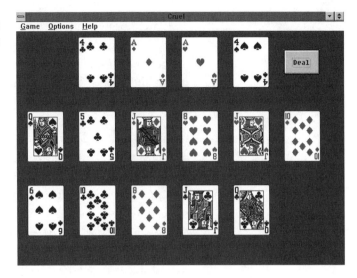

you can play the deuce of clubs on the ace of clubs. To move a card to a suit stack, drag it there or double-click the card you want to move. Move cards to the suit stacks whenever you can.

From one stack to another in the tableau. You can also move cards within the tableau, to change their order and to expose the cards hidden under the top cards of the tableau stacks. Move a card to another tableau stack if it's the same suit and one rank lower. For instance, you can play the three of hearts to the four of hearts, or the seven of diamonds to the eight of diamonds.

This figure gives you at least three possible moves among stacks in the tableau. See if you can find them. To move a card from one stack to another, drag it with the pointer.

Redealing. After you make all the moves you can, click the Deal button. The computer picks up the tableau stacks and deals them out again in stacks of four until it runs out of cards. You need to have moved at least one card to the suit stacks or from one stack to another in the tableau for the Deal button to work. The redeal usually exposes some of the cards previously hidden under the top cards of the stacks.

Cruel doesn't shuffle the cards before it deals them, so the order is unchanged. This lets you build up runs of cards in the tableau stacks, which makes it easier to move cards to the suit stacks. If a run contains more than four cards, they appear in two adjacent stacks when you redeal.

Options. Cruel doesn't have a lot of options. As in Solitaire, you can change the backs of the cards by choosing Deck from the Options menu. (Card backs are described in the chapter on Solitaire on page 16.) You can't see the card backs in Cruel until you complete a suit stack: the last card flips over to show that the stack is "closed." This can be kind of fun. If you choose one of the card backs that does something, you can see it happen on several stacks at once.

You can also turn the error messages on and off by choosing Messages from the Options menu. That's about it.

Endgame. When you win, a dialog box appears congratulating you on your victory. Pat yourself on the back and click on the OK button to make it go away. To play again, choose New from the Game menu or press F2.

Cruel lets you know when you've reached a stalemate. At the bottom of the tableau it says "Game Over - *xx* cards left."

To quit Cruel, double-click on the button at the top-left corner of the game window.

Scoring and Winning

You win at Cruel if you can move all the cards up to the suit stacks. You lose if you can't play any more cards among tableau stacks or to the suit stacks. Cruel keeps a cumulative record of your wins and losses, along with your highest and lowest number of remaining cards and your average score. You can see the record by choosing Record from the Game menu. If you want to start with a clean slate, choose Clear Scores from the Game Records dialog box.

Tips, Traps, and Sneaky Tricks

When you start the game, first check the tableau for deuces. Move any you find to the suit stacks right away. Then check for threes, and then higher cards that you can legally move to the suit stacks.

When you've exhausted the suit-stack possibilities, a good strategy is to start looking for runs of the higher-ranked cards, such as the king-queen-jack of any one suit. If you begin with the lower-ranked cards, you may block some good possible moves from one tableau stack to another.

It's also a good idea to move cards from stacks as close to the top-left corner of the tableau as you can. The game starts dealing the cards from the top-left stack in the tableau, so adding or taking away a card from the first stack changes the top card in all stacks after that. By the same token, it's not a good idea to get stuck making changes to the last few stacks in the tableau, because doing that only changes a couple of the stacks.

You can undo your moves, a card at a time, all the way back to the last time the cards were redealt. Choose Backup from the Game menu or press Backspace.

Cruel doesn't have many ways to cheat. There aren't any back doors into it, no fancy combinations of keys that let you shuffle cards, and no way to circumvent the scoring mechanism. However, you can peek under cards by making a move and then backing up. You can even run through the entire possible set of moves by holding down the Backspace key until all the cards are back in place. Then play just the cards you want. This isn't a lot, but it's enough to give you a little edge.

Golf

olf looks awfully simple, but you rapidly discover that it's simply awful. Ken Sykes (who also wrote the aptly named Cruel) decided to make a Windows version of Golf after he saw it on a roommate's computer. In the original card game, the idea was to try to beat "par" by minimizing "strokes" as you played through the nine "holes." Golf has no balls or clubs, although you may discover that you want to club the computer (or perhaps even Ken) every so often.

Object of the Game

The object of Golf is to move all the cards from the seven columns in the tableau at the top of the game window to the discard pile at the bottom. You do that by building runs on the discard pile with cards one higher or one lower in rank than the last discard played. (For definitions of card-game terms, see the chapter on Solitaire, page 18.)

Game Window

Golf starts with a tableau of seven columns and a stock of the remaining cards in the deck. Each column in the tableau contains five cards, all face up. The stock is at the bottom-left corner of the window. The number of cards left in the stock appears immediately below the stock. The discard pile starts just to the right of the stock.

Basic Golf layout

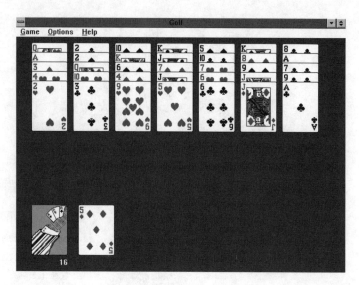

Play!

Starting the game. Click on the Golf icon in the Entertainment Pack group window. Windows loads Golf and immediately deals the first game for you, with the first card of the stock face up on the discard pile.

Moves. Golf gives you only one kind of move: tableau to discard pile. Move by clicking the bottom card (in other words, one that's fully exposed) of one of the tableau columns. If it's a legal card, it snaps instantly to the discard pile. The number below the discard pile changes to reflect the number of cards left in the stock. If you try to move an illegal card, the computer says "Not adjacent to card on pile." Click on OK to continue the game.

A legal card is one that's at the bottom of any tableau column and one rank higher or lower than the top card on the discard pile. A legal card can be any suit or color.

The implications of this rule are more interesting than they might seem at first. You can make runs in any suit, going up and down in rank, as long as you can get to a tableau card that's one rank higher or lower than the last one you put on the discard pile. You can reverse directions

Golf game in progress

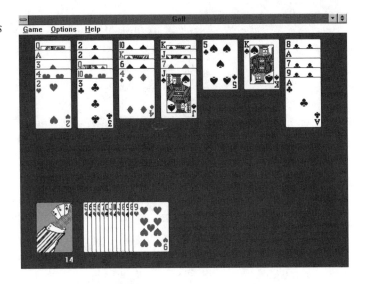

as many times as you like. For example, you can play 5-4-5-6-7-8-7-8-7-8-9-8-7 to the discard pile. If you're really lucky.

Golf places a couple of significant limitations on your moves from tableau to discard pile. First, you can't play a card on a king. That means you can't play a sequence such as 10-J-Q-K-Q-J, but you can play it as 10-J-Q-J-Q-K. Nor can you "wrap around" in a run of cards: J-Q-K-A-2 is illegal. The ace has a value of one in this game, and you can only play it on a deuce. For instance, if there's an ace on the discard pile, you can play a deuce, a three, another deuce, and then another ace. Similarly, you can only play the king on a queen. Therefore, when you play a king, your next card has to come from the stock.

When you can't play any more cards from the tableau, click the right mouse button to flip the next card from the stock to the discard pile. Continue flipping until you get a card on which you can play an exposed card from the tableau.

Options. Golf is a little thin on options. As in Solitaire and Cruel, you can change the backs of the cards by choosing

Deck from the Options menu, then picking the card back you want (see page 16). If you don't want the error messages to appear, choose Messages from the Options menu. When the check mark disappears, Messages is turned off.

Endgame. You win if you move all the cards to the discard pile. You lose if you can't play any more cards from the tableau to the discard pile. (You'll become abundantly familiar with losing at Golf.) To play another game, choose New from the Game menu or press F2. To quit, double-click on the button at the top-left corner of the Golf window.

Scoring and Winning

Scoring in Golf is easy. When you use up all the cards in the stock, the computer tells you the game's over. It also lets you know how many cards were left over in the tableau. (If you don't see the message at the bottom of the window, it means that there's still a possible move.) Your score is the number of cards still in the tableau when you run out of cards in the stock. As in Cruel, you can keep track of how you're doing by choosing Record from the Game menu. Record gives you the awful truth about the number of wins and the number of losses (and how disgusting the losses were). Don't get too excited if you see a bunch of nice high numbers, because the Golf scoring scheme is the opposite of the scheme in most games—you want your scores as *low* as you can get them. Clear the old scores by clicking on Clear Scores.

From the keyboard

Golf gives you only a few keyboard options. To start a new game, press F2. To get Help, press F1. To undo or back up a move, press Backspace. To shrink the game window to an icon, press Esc.

You can't move the cards without a mouse.

Winning in Golf doesn't get you anything fancy—just a simple dialog box with the message "Congratulations!" Consider this a major award even if cards don't start leaping all over the screen. Winning more than one game in 50 is good playing. Click on OK to clear your kudos from the window.

Tips, Traps, and Sneaky Tricks

From the tableau columns, choose cards that let you discard long sequences of other cards—the longer the better. The more cards you can discard before having to flip from the stock, the better your chances of winning. You want to keep as many cards in the stock as you can until you absolutely need them.

If you have a choice and you're getting to the tops of the columns, try to keep several columns active. It's a lot easier to clear cards from a couple of columns than from a single column.

When you have a good chance to win, it helps to hold a queen in reserve if you'll have to play a king eventually. The only way to play that king is on a queen. Likewise, keep a deuce around for that last ace.

The best strategy is to plan each sequence of cards before you begin moving cards to the discard pile. But sometimes the cards just don't play out the way you planned, in which case the Backup option from the Game menu is your best friend. You can play a sequence, back up, and replay it until you find the best approach. There's no penalty for backing the game up as far as you want to go and replaying the whole thing over again. You can back up to the beginning of the game if you want to, which lets you cheat a little: you now know what the cards in the stock are.

CHAPTER 5

IdleWild

dleWild isn't really a game, but a set of "screen savers." When you leave your monitor on and idle for a long time, the image can burn into the screen permanently, appearing lightly over any subsequent image. IdleWild prevents that by changing the image on the screen to an animation whenever you ignore the computer for a few minutes.

When the Microsoft Entertainment Package developers approached Brad Christian about including his animated screen saver *Fireworks*, he offered instead a program that could run a selection of different animated images. With Tony Krueger, Brad wrote all the screen saver animations for the Windows Entertainment Pack, Volume One.

IdleWild is also included with the Windows Entertainment Pack, Volumes Two and Three. Each volume contains a different set of animations. The setup procedure included with each volume puts everything in the WEP directory. This gives each volume access to all the screen savers. For information about the screen savers in Volumes Two and Three, see the other IdleWild chapters later in this book.

How IdleWild Works

IdleWild only runs with Windows applications. It can't register idle time in a DOS application, even when Windows is running. IdleWild is also disabled during a Windows tutorial.

IdleWild doesn't affect the Windows application that's running; it just replaces the screen image. The application is restored to the screen as soon as you touch the mouse or the keyboard. IdleWild also alerts you if you've been staring blankly at the screen while your mind wanders. When fireworks or stars suddenly invade your monitor, it tends to snap you back to the present.

You set the length of time the computer waits before it runs IdleWild. You can turn it off temporarily by moving the pointer to the lower-right corner of the screen. You can also set the pointer to vanish after ten seconds of idleness, to keep the screen from looking cluttered (it reappears instantly when you touch or move the mouse again).

Activating IdleWild gives you instant privacy. By moving the pointer to the upper-right corner of the screen, you instantly run a screen saver. But you need to plan ahead. If you don't want people to see what you're doing, be sure to run one of the animations that completely replaces the screen image, such as *Fireworks*, instead of one that just breaks up the screen image, as *Shuffle* does.

Running IdleWild

To start IdleWild, double-click the IdleWild icon in the Entertainment Pack group window. The IdleWild window appears, in two sections. On the left are the names of the

Beware!

You may run into some problems with IdleWild if you install Volume One after you install Volume Two or Three. The executable IdleWild files in the last version you install automatically replace the existing IdleWild executable files. This means if you install IdleWild One after Two or Three, you won't have the latest and greatest executable files, and you'll lose the extra options included with Volumes Two and Three (Password, Hot Corners, and so on). To correct this, just install Volume Two or Three *after* you install Volume One.

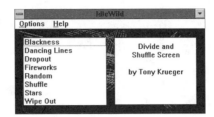

IdleWild startup window

available screen savers. A scroll bar on the side of this section lets you scroll to the screen savers that aren't currently visible. The section on the right lists information about the highlighted screen saver. IdleWild has two drop-down menus, Options, and Help. (A menu item is activated when a checkmark appears beside it.) The Options menu is the key to setting IdleWild the way you want it to run:

Options, Set Delay lets you set the length of time IdleWild waits before running a screen saver. Choose Set Delay from the Options menu. A dialog box appears. Type the length of the delay you want into the text field. (Type the numeral; if you type text, such as "ten," IdleWild doesn't recognize it as a legal value and gives you an error message.) One minute is the minimum time for a delay. If you set the delay to zero, IdleWild automatically resets it to five minutes. If you set it to less than zero or leave it empty, you get a message that says "Illegal value. Click OK to continue."

Options, Blank Pointer makes the pointer vanish when the mouse is idle for ten seconds. Any movement of the mouse makes the pointer reappear immediately.

Options, Autoload automatically loads IdleWild any time you open Windows. When Autoload is active, the mini-mized IdleWild icon appears in the corner of the screen as soon as you start Windows. This means you don't have to open IdleWild every time.

Options, Blank Now lets you activate any of the screen savers immediately. This is a great way to try the screen

Special FX   IdleWild can create some interesting effects. For example, if you have the minimum one-minute delay set, when you win at Solitaire, IdleWild blanks the screen while the cards are cascading. If you then move the mouse, the screen is restored with a solid green background rather than showing the patterns left by the cards that have already fallen. The cards continue to fall, but they seem to appear out of nowhere.

savers and see which ones you like. Use the arrow keys to highlight to the screen saver you want to see. Then choose Options, Blank Now or press Enter to run the screen saver. Move the mouse or press any key to return to IdleWild.

Options, Exit lets you leave IdleWild. This turns off Idle-Wild until you run it again.

Volume One Screen Savers

The IdleWild feature in Windows Entertainment Pack, Volume One, gives you a choice of eight animated images. Here's what each does:

Blackness   wipes everything from the screen and displays a black screen, as if your monitor is off.

Dancing Lines   draws colored lines that twist and tumble across the screen.

Dropout   has tiles fall from the screen and bounce off the edge (something like what happens when you win at Solitaire) until the entire screen is black. It then chooses a different animation to run on the screen.

Fireworks   gives you the Fourth of July on your screen. Rockets shoot up and explode, then cascade down.

Random   picks a screen animation at random and runs it.

Shuffle   divides the screen into squares and then moves the squares around. It's similar to the kids' toy that has the numerals 1 through 15 on small tiles. You'd move them by sliding them around until you got the numbers back in order. Shuffle uses several different square sizes when dividing the screen, so the effect is different each time it runs. Eventually, Shuffle chooses another screen saver to run.

Stars   is a trip through space. As you watch the screen you see stars passing you as you move toward some distant destination. "Ahead warp factor 9!"

Wipeout   clears the screen by moving in from one of five directions, the top of the screen, the bottom, right side, left side, or toward all four directions at once from a dot in the center of the screen. Once Wipeout has cleared the screen, it chooses another screen saver to run.

From the keyboard

After you double-click the IdleWild icon in the Entertainment Pack group window, you can run it entirely from the keyboard. Alt-O opens the Options menu. Alt-H opens the Help menu. To cycle through the menus, type Alt-O or Alt-H and then use the left or right arrow keys. Once you find the menu item you want, pick it by typing the underlined letter in the selection or use the up and down arrow keys to highlight it. Then press Enter.

Use the arrow keys to move up and down through the list of screen savers. To run one immediately, move the highlight onto it and press Enter. Pressing any key returns you to IdleWild.

CHAPTER 6

Minesweeper

ou'll either love Minesweeper or you'll hate it. You need a lot of logic and a little bit of luck to come out okay in the end. You need logic to figure out which squares cover deadly land mines. Luck comes in when you don't have enough information to tell which squares cover mines and which don't. All you can do is step on a square and see if you've guessed right. It takes only one miscalculation or one bad guess to take you out.

Minesweeper is especially nice if your office doesn't have much privacy. The game window for the Beginner level is small and inconspicuous, and the game is *silent*.

Object of the Game

Your mission is to make the minefield safe for your platoon by uncovering all the squares that don't hide mines. The game is timed, so you have to move quickly to beat the best time for the level you're playing.

Game Window

Minesweeper's layout is a simple gray grid with eight squares on a side. Under any square may lurk a land mine just waiting for you to set it off and blast you into oblivion. The mines are already hidden when you open the game.

The counter in the upper-left corner of the Mine-sweeper window lets you keep track of the mines you think you've discovered. At the beginning of the game it shows

*Game window
before play begins*

how many mines are hidden on the field. When you mark a square you think covers a mine, the number decreases by one. Beware—the count doesn't mean you're right in figuring out where a mine is hidden; it just means you've marked a square. The count goes to negative numbers when you mark more squares than there are mines.

The counter in the upper-right corner of the window is the timer. It starts when you make your first move and keeps track of the seconds it takes you to clear the minefield—or blow yourself to kingdom come.

Minesweeper gives you only two menus at the top of the game window: Game and Help. The Game menu lets you restart a game, choose a skill level, set color in the window, and check the score record. (You *can* play this game with a monochrome monitor.) The Help menu gives you access to Minesweeper's Help screens.

Finally, the happy face between the mine counter and the timer is a general who watches you and reacts to your progress. When you win, he slips on some shades to let you know how truly cool you are. When you lose, he frowns. And when you uncover a square—well, try it and see.

Play!

Starting the game.

Start Minesweeper by double-clicking on the Minesweeper icon in the Entertainment Pack group window. The Minesweeper window opens to the Beginner level. The field looks safe enough, but it hides ten deadly mines, wired in series to go off all at once when you step on only one mine.

*The general is
watching you.*

Moves.

Minesweeper gives you three kinds of moves. First, you can uncover a "safe" square—one that doesn't hide a mine. Second, you can mark a square that you're pretty sure *does* hide a mine, so you can't set it off. Third, you can uncover a whole area of safe squares.

Your first step is always safe.

What a "whoosh" looks like.

A marked mine

You're guaranteed to live through your first step onto the minefield. It's the second one that can be dangerous. To uncover a square, click on it. If it's a safe square, a number appears in it, telling you how many of its eight adjacent squares hide mines. (If it's not safe, you and your platoon buy the farm.)

If you're lucky, your first move will give you a "whoosh" where uncovering just one square can open up a whole area of safe squares on the field. When you uncover a square that isn't next to a mine, the computer automatically uncovers all the surrounding blank squares. A square with no mines next to it has no number in it. Sometimes the game clears a large area but leaves one lone covered square somewhere in the middle. That's a mine, sure as anything.

Compare the number in an uncovered square to the number of covered squares touching it. If the number in a square is equal to the number of adjacent covered squares, you know that all the covered squares hide mines. This is most evident when a square with a 1 on it touches only one covered square.

To play it safe, you should mark the squares that you're pretty sure hide mines. Do that by right-clicking the suspicious square. A flag appears on the square. To get rid of the flag, right-click on it again. Once you mark a square, it's safe—you can't step on it. (Clicking on it with the left button has no effect when the square is marked.) Every time you mark a square, the number in the mine counter at the upper-left corner of the window decreases by one.

If you're really unsure whether a square hides a mine, mark it with a question mark. Turn on the question-mark option by choosing Marks(?) from the Game menu, then double-click on the square you want to mark. Turn off the question-mark option by choosing Marks(?) again. (A check mark shows next to the option when it's turned on.) Remember, the question mark is just a reminder. It doesn't make the square safe, because you can still uncover the square by clicking on it. Nor does it affect the mine counter.

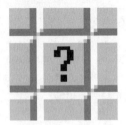

Maybe it's a mine;
maybe it isn't…

The third kind of move lets you uncover all the safe squares surrounding an uncovered square. On an uncovered, numbered square with some adjacent covered squares and one or more adjacent squares flagged, click the left and right mouse buttons together. If all the adjacent uncovered, unmarked squares are safe, they'll all be uncovered at the same time. If you put a flag on a square that doesn't really hide a mine, all the mines explode and you lose. If you marked one or more squares correctly but didn't mark all the squares that hide a mine, the surrounding squares show up blank for an instant, but they aren't uncovered. That way you know that more mines lurk in the vicinity. This is a great way to speed up your time, but it really takes practice to do it right.

Remember, this stunt won't work on a covered square. And it's pointless to do it on an uncovered square where all the adjacent squares are uncovered, too.

Skill levels.

The Game menu lets you choose a skill level. At the Beginner level, you get an eight-by-eight layout with ten hidden mines. The Intermediate level is sixteen-by-sixteen with forty mines, and the Expert is sixteen-by-thirty, with ninety-nine mines.

From the keyboard

Minesweeper doesn't have many keyboard shortcuts, aside from the keyboard menu commands noted in the Introduction to this book. You can get Help with F1, start a new game with F2, access the menus with Alt-F3, quit with Alt-F4, and toggle Sound on and off with Alt-F5 (if you've used the special trick in the "Tips, Traps, and Sneaky Tricks" part of this chapter to turn it on). This game doesn't have an Undo feature, and you can't stop the timer to think a while.

Better luck next time.

You can also design your own layout by choosing the Game Custom option from the Game menu. Type in the dimensions for the layout and the number of mines you want to hide. Be careful to keep your numbers in reasonable proportion with the size of the field, though. If you have a ten-by-ten layout, you won't do too well with eighty mines.

On a Custom board, the lowest number of squares you can have is eight-by-eight. You can have no fewer than ten mines on any size board. The maximum board height is twenty-four; maximum width is thirty. The various layouts put natural limits on the number of mines you can place. For example, if you define a ten-by-ten layout and call for ninety-nine mines, the computer changes that number to eighty-one, the maximum allowed in that layout. Minesweeper doesn't track best scores for the Custom skill level.

Now, for a really short game, try 667 mines on a thirty-by-twenty-four field—you won't last more than two moves.

Endgame.
Make a few random moves. If you mess up and uncover a mine, it and all the other mines explode. You and your platoon are hamburger. If you marked a square that *didn't* cover a mine, a red "X" appears over it. The game's over.

When you win, the general beams at you and you can start another game. If you have the best time for your skill level, the computer asks you your name, so it can record you as the new high scorer.

Start another game by choosing Start game from the Game menu or clicking the happy face. (If you're *really* lazy, just press the F2 key.) To quit Minesweeper, choose Exit from the Game menu, or double-click the top-left button on the game window.

Scoring and Winning

In Minesweeper, you either win or lose. The game doesn't award points. To be a real hero in Minesweeper, not only do you have to clear the field of mines, but you have to do

You did it!

it *fast*. The computer tracks your playing time in seconds. The game is the most fun when you compete with other players to see who can clear the field in the best time. Keep in mind that you can win this game even if you don't mark all the mines.

When you win with a best time for that skill level, and the computer asks you for your name, it also tells you who that last high scorer was. If no one has set a record yet for that level, the last high scorer is Anonymous.

After you type your name, click OK or press Enter to add your new time to the scoreboard. The computer then shows you the best times for all levels. You can see the game record any time you want by choosing Best Times from the Game menu. To reset the best times, click Reset Scores and OK in the display box.

Tips, Traps, and Sneaky Tricks

If you're still with us after your first few moves on the field, look at the numbered squares that touch the marked (mined) squares. See if they're touching a number of marked squares equal to the numeral on the square. If they are, you know that all the other adjacent squares are safe (unless you made a mistake in your logic), and you can uncover them.

Remember that mine-marking is just a convenience, a tool to help you keep track. You can save time by *not* marking mines that are obvious anyway, such as the ones lurking in the middle of a large cleared area.

Your strategy should be different for different skill levels. At the easy level, it pays to guess randomly near the edges and corners. In fact, guessing a corner successfully can clear out a quarter of the board if the mines are near the center. At higher skill levels all you can do is start by guessing randomly. With the larger concentrations of mines, large empty areas are less frequent.

Sometimes when you try to click a corner for an opening move, the mouse shifts slightly and clicks a square nearby.

If this happens, leave well enough alone. For some reason, the mouse is inclined to avoid a corner that hides a mine during the first move.

Remember that the object is to uncover all of the squares that are not mines, not to mark all of the squares that are. If you've neared the end of a game and you're left with two squares, one of which is a mine and one of which isn't, uncover the one that isn't rather than marking the one that is. If you guess right, it might make your time a little lower.

It's possible to have sound with Minesweeper, if you want it. To activate the sound option, use File Manager to edit the file ENTPACK.INI. Under the section labeled [Minesweeper], add a line that says "Sound=3." When Sound is activated in this way, you get a series of beeps when you explode a mine and a tune plays when you win.

The spy in the corner

Robert Donner, author of Minesweeper, planted a spy in the upper-left corner of your screen. You can't see him, but he'll flash a light to let you know where the mines are if you give him the password.

Here's how to do that. First of all, move all of your windows over so that the upper-left corner of the screen is empty. (Donner's spy is easiest to see if you have a solid-color desktop, so you may want to reset your desktop to a dark color if you've been running a pattern there.) Open a new copy of Minesweeper. Before you do anything else, move the cursor onto the minefield, then type "xyzzy" and press Enter. Now press Shift; then move the mouse a hair. You should be able to see a tiny white dot (a single pixel) in the upper-left corner of your screen. That's the spy's signal light. As long as you are on a safe square, his light stays on; as soon as you move onto a square that hides a mine, the light goes out. With the spy in the corner, you'll always be able to get through the minefield without any casualties.

The best hint on how to beat the game comes from Ralph Lipe. "One way to cheat in the Minesweeper game is to start the game, then minimize it and start another copy of Minesweeper. (Click on the icon in the window, not the minimized version). This won't really start another copy— it restores the original mines, but the clock has stopped and won't start again. You can win at expert level in 1 second!" Of course, after that it's hard to beat your best time.

CHAPTER 7

Pegged

 f you've ever stopped in at a truck stop in the wee hours for biscuits and gravy, you've probably seen the wood-and-golf-tee version of Pegged. Pegged is a puzzle game of strategy and logic, attributed to a prisoner in the Bastille. After a few games, you'll know if there's a connection between the Bastille and America's truck stops.

Object of the Game

The object of the game is to remove pegs, leaving a single peg in the center of the pegboard—simple, direct, difficult.

Game Window

The pegboard is cross-shaped, with three-dimensional holes. Depending on the pattern you choose from the Options menu, a few, some, or all but one of the holes have pegs in them at the start of the game. The illustration shows the default pattern.

Play!

Starting the game. Click on the Pegged icon in the Entertainment Pack group window. The Pegged game window appears, ready to play. The game defaults to the Cross pattern, with only six pegs.

Moves. The Cross version of Pegged is pretty easy. Drag one of the pegs horizontally or vertically to a vacant hole in the

Cross layout in Pegged

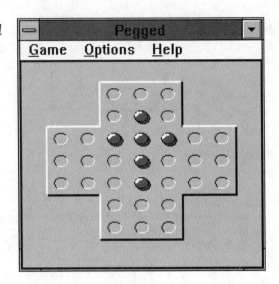

pegboard, jumping over one other peg in the process. The peg you jumped automatically disappears from the board. (This is like jumping a piece in a game of checkers.) Now keep jumping until only one peg is left or you can't jump any more. Diagonal moves aren't allowed.

Skill levels. The pattern you see the first time you load Pegged is the Cross. You can choose a new pattern from the Options menu by clicking on the pattern name. There are seven patterns: the Cross, the Plus, the Fireplace, the Up Arrow, the Pyramid, the Diamond, and Solitaire. The patterns start easy and get progressively harder.

Endgame. When you win, the computer congratulates you. Click on OK to get the dialog box to go away. As soon as

From the keyboard

You need a mouse to move the pegs on the pegboard, but you can use the keys to issue commands. F1 gets you to the Help screens, and the Backspace key lets you undo previous moves. You can try the same pegboard pattern again by pressing F2. To shrink the game window to an icon, press Esc.

you can't jump any more pegs, the computer says "Game Over." Again, click on the OK button to clear the screen and go on to something else. To start a new game, choose New from the Game menu or click F2. To quit Pegged, double-click on the button at the top-left corner of the game window.

Scoring and Winning

Pegged is one of the few Windows games that doesn't keep score for you. Either you win the game or you don't—and you're the only person who will ever know which it was.

Tips, Traps, and Sneaky Tricks

When you're first learning Pegged, play the patterns in the order they're listed in the Options menu. The winning moves for one pattern are based on the winning moves for one or more of the previous patterns. On some of the harder games, it helps to move the pegs into the starting pattern of a preceding game. If you find that you're stumped by one pattern, try going back to the previous pattern for a clue.

A basic rule of thumb is to move the pegs toward the center of the pegboard, as any pegs left alone in the wings are hard, if not impossible, to play.

You can back the game up as many moves as you want any time during or after the game by choosing Backup from the Game menu. Pressing Backspace does the same thing.

The online Help for Pegged has some interesting variations for final patterns from the Solitaire level. Instead of ending up with one peg in the center at the end of the game, you try to get a square, a wall, or a pinwheel for the final pattern. These patterns aren't any easier than the standard game, but they are fun and they make a pleasant change.

There's no way to cheat at Pegged. You're going to have to work for this one.

CHAPTER 8

Taipei

aipei is a stepchild of the ancient Chinese game, mah jongg, which is kind of like rummy played with wooden or bone tiles instead of cards. We don't really know where mah jongg came from or when it was invented, but Chinese folklore suggests that for centuries it was played only by royalty, who kept it a secret from commoners. Other legends tell us that a Chinese general invented the game to keep his troops occupied during a long siege, or that sailors played it to ward off seasickness. Dominoes, another Chinese game, may have been a precursor of mah jongg.

Taipei is a solitaire version of mah jongg. The computer starts the game by laying out the pieces. Winning is always possible, but seldom easy.

Object of the Game

To win at Taipei, you have to remove all the tiles from the board by clicking on matching pairs of free tiles. You lose when there are no more untrapped pairs to take away. Taipei tells your fortune when you win. One snappy example goes something like this: "You will be invited to a party where strange customs prevail."

Game Window

The Taipei game window is a small rectangular play area with a seemingly random arrangement of picture tiles on

Standard layout in Taipei

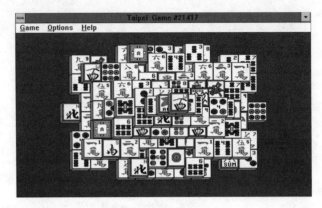

it. The tile layout shown here is called Standard, which comes up when you first play Taipei. You can choose from a variety of layouts, but this chapter mostly talks about the Standard layout. The layouts are in three dimensions (you'll see this better on a VGA monitor).

You can use the Game menu to start a new game, choose a specific game by its number, get a hint, start the same game again, make the computer play by itself, or quit Taipei. From the Options menu you can pick a board layout and turn the Color and Messages options on or off.

A few words about the tiles. The patterns on the tiles look sort of random the first time you see them, but they're

Who writes these things, anyway?

In the original computer version of Taipei, the winning fortunes were written more for humor than for good taste. A new set of fortunes was needed for the version to be shipped, but the schedule got short, and universally offensive fortunes were still to be found. An ingenious programmer made a quick trip to a nearby wholesale food store and bought a huge bag of fortune cookies. Caught between a deadline and an office full of crumbs, desperate programmers typed in the fortunes. That's why when you win the game you may see the same fortune you got at your favorite Chinese restaurant last night. Believe in it.

The One of Bamboo

not. Each tile is one of four basic types: Suit tiles, Honors tiles, Flower tiles, and Season tiles. The Suit tiles are further divided into Bamboos, Characters, and Dots.

The Bamboos sport green pieces of bamboo and a small numeral. (If you have a black-and-white monitor, you'll *really* have a tough time telling the tile types apart!) By the way, the One of Bamboo has neither a "one" nor bamboo on it. It has a single colorful bird.

Bamboo

The Characters have a red pagoda design, a blue Chinese character, and the number of the tile.

Chinese characters

The Dots have multicolored circles with the corresponding numeral on all except the one-dot tile, which just has a single large circle.

Dots

The Suit tiles range from 1 to 9 in each suit. There are four tiles of each number and suit.

The Honors tiles are divided into Winds and Dragons. The four Winds have a black Chinese character and the first letter of the wind's direction (for example, the North Wind tile has an "N" in the top-right corner). There are four Winds tiles (two pairs) for each Wind.

Winds

Taipei has three kinds of Dragon tiles: Red, Green, and White. The Red Dragon tile has a big red Chinese character and the Green Dragon tile has a big green one. The White Dragon has a black box design on it. Taipei has two pairs of each of the three Dragons in each layout.

Dragons

Each Season and Flower tile has a different picture and the name of a flower or a season on it. Each layout has only four Season tiles and four Flower tiles.

Seasons and flowers

Play!

Starting the game. Double-click on the Taipei icon in the Entertainment Pack group window to start Taipei. Taipei opens with the word TAIPEI written in pseudo-Oriental characters across the game window. To start a game, choose New from the Game menu or press F2.

All Taipei games are winnable, and there are thousands to choose from. Each is numbered, so you can go back to the ones you're especially fond of. Game numbers appear in the title bar across the top of each game.

To start a certain game, choose Select Game from the Game menu. Click in the text box and type the number of the game you want to play. Click OK or press Enter.

Moves. The challenge of Taipei is to find matching pairs of free tiles and take them off the board. Tiles match when they have exactly the same pattern and number. The only exceptions are Seasons and Flowers: any two Season tiles match, and any two Flower tiles match.

To choose a tile, just click on it. If the tile is free, its color changes. Now click on a matching tile. If the second tile is free, the matching pair disappears from the board.

The pointer tells you if a tile is free by changing from an arrow to a cross. If you click on a tile that isn't free, the computer beeps and displays an annoying message box. Click on OK to make it go away.

A tile is free if no other tile touches it on its right or left sides. (Top or bottom are okay).

If you choose a tile by mistake, you can cancel the selection by clicking it a second time.

Hints. If you need a hint, choose Hint from the Game menu or press H on the keyboard. If you don't like the first hint Taipei offers, ask for another; you can keep doing this until the computer has shown you all the free pairs. When you've seen all the free pairs, the first free pair reappears.

Undoing a move. To cancel a lousy move, choose Back-up from the Game menu or press the Backspace key. This works for any number of moves, so if you really want to, you can retrace your steps through a game and start again from

From the keyboard

Taipei gives you only a few keyboard shortcuts. Press F2 to start a new game. Press Backspace to back up the game move by move. You can get a hint for the next move by pressing the H key, and Help by pressing F1.

You can't move the tiles without a mouse.

Pressing Esc clears the game off the screen.

any point. You can even use these keys if the "No Tiles Free" message has appeared; click on OK and then back up to the place where you want to start again.

Autoplay. The Autoplay option on the Game menu tells the computer to play the game for you. There are a couple of problems with this little cheat, however. First, the computer plays so fast that you can't follow the action. Second, and worse, the computer isn't a very good player. It grabs tiles by pairs, but it doesn't do it strategically, so it sometimes loses a game you might have won if you'd played on your own. You can sometimes rescue a game that the computer has lost by backing up a few moves to an obviously stupid one, making a better move, and then turning the computer loose again. Stop Autoplay by choosing it again from the Game menu.

When you use Autoplay you don't get to see a fortune unless you pull the last pair of tiles yourself. To get your unearned fortune, let the computer play all the way to the last pair of tiles, then interrupt it and play them yourself.

Skill levels. Taipei has seven different layouts: Standard, Bridge, Castle, Cube, Glyph, Pyramid, and Spiral. The Cube is the easiest to win. Pyramid and Glyph are fairly easy; Bridge, Castle, and Standard are harder (mostly because it's hard to tell which level the tiles are on). For sheer irritation value, try Spiral. This layout spreads the tiles all over the window and makes it very hard to see pairs. The illustration shows the Bridge layout.

Options. The Options menu lets you customize the game.

Color. When the opening Taipei screen appears, take a look at the Options menu to make sure the Color option is active, if you have a color monitor. (Any menu item is active when a check mark appears beside it.) Turn it off if you have a monochrome monitor or want to play with black and white tiles (like going into a boxing match with both hands tied behind your back).

Bridge layout in Taipei

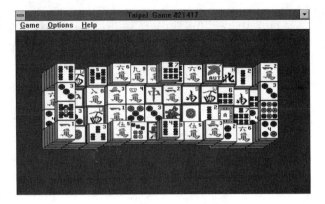

Messages. When the Messages option is active, Taipei displays an error message every time you try to make an illegal move. It's a bore and a pain, and the game goes faster if you turn this option off. Even with Messages off, Taipei tells you when you have no more legal moves, and it still gives you a fortune when you win the game.

Endgame. When you win, Taipei tells your fortune. When you lose, the computer says "No free tiles." If you want to see how close you came to winning, you can drag the dialog box aside and see the remaining tiles. You can also use the Backup or Start Over commands on the Game menu to replay part or all of the same game.

To quit Taipei, click Exit on the Game menu or double-click the top-left corner of the game window.

Scoring and Winning

Taipei doesn't score your performance or keep track of your speed. You win if you manage to get all the tiles off the board. You lose when there's a stack of tiles left and you can't make any more legal moves.

Tips, Traps, and Sneaky Tricks

The most satisfying way to play Taipei is to approach it the way you play chess, weighing the values of several options and looking as many moves ahead as you can.

Not every game uses all the tiles

In order to make the layout work, some pairs of tiles are omitted at random. Castle and Standard use all the tiles, but Bridge, Cube, Glyph, Pyramid, and Spiral do not.

Take off the top tiles as soon as possible. The top tile in the Standard game blocks about half the tiles in the layout. If you can't pair it off, you'll get stuck pretty fast. The Standard layout also has a single tile on each side, each of which blocks the ends of two rows. Get rid of these tiles early, if you can.

Although the object of Taipei is to get all the tiles off the board, it may not be best to blast a pair of tiles as soon as you discover it. The other tiles in the set might be in a column, with one blocking the other. If you take the first available pair, you may not be able to unblock the second pair. To avoid this trap, try waiting until you can locate three or four matching tiles. When all four tiles are free, get rid of them immediately. If no set of tiles has all four visible, find a set with three of the four free. Go first for the tiles that are blocking adjacent tiles or covering hidden tiles.

Whenever you have a choice about which tiles to remove, take the ones that give you the most new options.

The Glyph of Bogosity

You'll find a rather unusual message in the Taipei Help files if you double-click on the highlighted word "Glyph" in the Help screens under Options Menu Help. (Press F1 and click on Options Menu.) Dave Norris, the author of Taipei, was an avid Dungeons and Dragons player for years. He and his cronies used to use the term "Glyph of Bogosity" to describe a magic item that didn't work the way it was supposed to. What started as a joke became a game standard, and the Glyph appeared regularly in other games as a codeword signifying a blooper, blunder, bungle, snafu, or anything that didn't work as expected.

CHAPTER 9

TETRIS

TETRIS is a puzzle in motion, an exciting (and highly addictive) game of strategy and quick thinking. The original version was the demonic invention of Alexy Pazhitnov and Vadim Gerasimov of the USSR Academy of Sciences Computer Center in Moscow. From the Soviet Union, the game found its way to Western Europe and finally to the US. TETRIS was first released here on the Macintosh by Spectrum HoloByte. Then Microsoft's Dave Edson wrote the Windows version as a programming exercise while he was a co-op student. Spectrum HoloByte wasn't interested in buying the Windows version at the time, so Microsoft used it for this Entertainment Pack.

Object of the Game

Brightly colored blocks fall from the top of the play area. You must rotate and move the irregularly shaped pieces as they fall so they fit together at the bottom, with no gaps. When you complete a row, it vanishes, giving you points and more room to manipulate new pieces as they fall. The object is to earn as many points as possible before you mess up completely and the game ends.

Game Window

The TETRIS game window consists of a brightly patterned background (the pattern changes as you ascend to higher

TETRIS starting screen

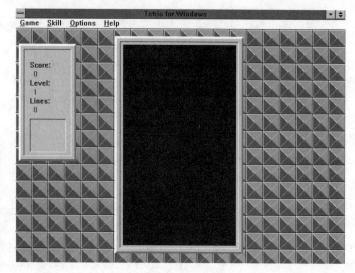

Right pothook

Left pothook

Right L

Left L

Blivet

Square

Straight Line

skill levels) with a vertical black rectangle in the center. The black area is where you stack the blocks. The box at the upper-left of the window shows your current score, the skill level, and the number of lines or rows you've finished so far. The blocks come in seven shapes: left pothook, right pothook, left L, right L, blivet, square, and straight line.

Just below the title bar are four menus. Use these to start the game or suspend it temporarily, set options and skill levels, get to the Help windows, and check on best scores.

Play!

Starting the game. Click on the TETRIS icon in the Entertainment Pack group window to start the game. TETRIS opens with a credits screen over the play area—click on the OK button to get rid of it. To start the game, choose New from the Game menu or press F2. The first falling piece soon appears at the top of the play area.

Moves. Use the arrow keys to rotate pieces or move them left and right as they fall. The idea is to get each piece to fit neatly with the others that are already at the bottom of the play area. Don't leave gaps if you can help it.

To move a piece horizontally, press the left or right arrow key. To rotate a piece, press the up arrow key, or the 5 key on the numeric pad. After you've rotated the piece correctly and it's directly above where you want it to land, press the down arrow or the Insert key. The piece drops and the next piece starts to fall.

With the first few pieces, try to fill up as much of the bottom row as possible. Work your way in from the borders and leave the middle free, as in the illustration here.

Skill levels. After you finish a certain number of rows, you qualify for the next skill level. The background changes, the level indicator at the left of the screen goes up one, and, most importantly, the pieces start falling faster. This happens each time you go up a level. (If it's any consolation, the pieces don't speed up as they get closer to the bottom; they fall at a constant rate.)

To crank up the skill level, choose Starting Level from the Skill menu, then pick the skill level that challenges you. The pieces fall faster the higher you go. If you're feeling muy macho, you can start the game with up to nine rows of randomly scattered pieces. Choose Starting Rows from the Skill menu, then pick the number of rows you want.

Playing TETRIS with two players. You can play TETRIS competition-style. Choose 2 Player from the Options menu. The window changes to display two play areas.

The player on the right uses the arrow keys, as usual. The player on the left uses keys on the main part of the

Use the numeric keypad

Although you can play the basic game with just the up, down, left, and right arrow keys, you should use the numeric keypad rather than the T-shaped arrow keypad. One variation of TETRIS described later in this chapter uses the 1 and 3 keys on the numeric pad, and you'll have trouble shifting over if you get used to the T-shaped pad.

TETRIS game in progress

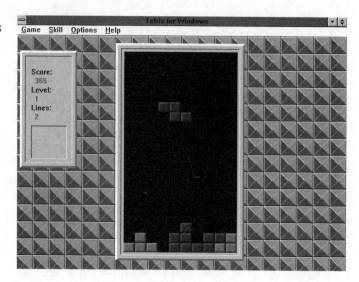

keyboard: the J to move left, the L to move right, the K to rotate, and the spacebar to drop the game pieces.

To play cutthroat TETRIS with two players, choose Penalize Other Player from the Options menu. When you finish two or more rows, the other player has that many rows of random pieces added to the bottom of their rows. This can seriously hamper your opponent's ability to move or rotate pieces.

Endgame. The game is over when the pieces are stacked to the top of the play area. You get a Game Over message in a dialog box. Click on OK to continue. If your score is high enough, you are inducted into the TETRIS Hall of Fame. You can enter your cool name and cool quote. These appear side by side, next to your score, on a chart of TETRIS experts. Click on OK to get back to the TETRIS screen.

From the keyboard

TETRIS is one of the few games in the Microsoft Entertainment Packs that you have to play with the keyboard. To start a new game, press F2. To pause or restart a game, press F3. To get help, press F1. To back up a move, press Backspace. To shrink the game window, press Esc.

Two-player TETRIS
game in progress

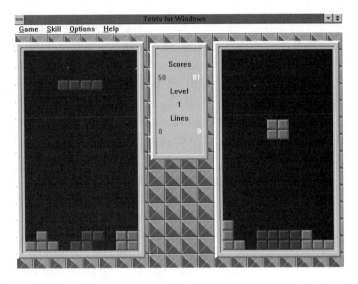

Two-player TETRIS ends when either player's stack fills up. The winner is the person with the highest score.

Start a new game by choosing New from the Game menu or by pressing F2. Quit TETRIS by double-clicking the button at the top-left corner of the game window. Then click on OK.

Scoring and Winning

With TETRIS, the idea is to rack up as many points as possible before the game ends. The number of points you earn is largely a function of how few times you move or rotate each piece and how soon you can drop it. Each time you move or rotate a piece, it's worth fewer points. As you ascend to higher skill levels, the number of points per piece increases. You also get points for removing rows of blocks: 100 points for one row, 200 points for two rows, 400 points for three rows, and 800 points for four rows.

Tips, Traps, and Sneaky Tricks

Before you start the first game, turn on Piece Preview in the Options menu. This gives you an advance peek at the upcoming piece, which gives you more time to think through your next move. If you had Piece Preview turned on in your previous game, the first piece that appears in the new game is the last piece shown in the Piece Preview box.

Don't build mountains of pieces. Mountains make it difficult to move pieces from one side of the play area to the other. Keep the top of your rows as level as you can. By the same token, don't create one- or two-block-wide canyons more than two rows deep. If you do, you either have to wait for a long, skinny piece or use a smaller piece that leaves a gap, which will be hard to dig out. Finally, try to maintain one flat spot three blocks wide, to set wide, flat pieces on.

If a falling piece is close to another piece or the edge of the play area, you may not be able to rotate it. First, move it away and then rotate it.

You don't have to fill rows in any order. It's a good idea to finish a row whenever you can so that the game removes it, but don't wait for just the right piece (usually one of the long, skinny ones) to come along to complete four rows at once. Use an L-shaped piece to take out a few rows and then do it again. You need to keep the number of rows down as far as possible to give you the most time and space to maneuver subsequent falling pieces.

Sometimes you just won't get the piece you need to fill in a row. If necessary, you can leave a space in the stacked pieces, then come back to fill that space in when you complete the rows above it. This strategy helps you gain points by removing completed rows, and it also helps to flatten out some of the hills and valleys you may have created in the process.

Training wheels

The Piece Preview option is very handy for learning to play TETRIS, but it reduces your score. Treat it like a set of training wheels on a bicycle, and stop using it as soon as you get used to the game.

If you have an overhang, you can slip a piece underneath it by letting the piece drift down and then pressing the left or right arrow at the last moment before it settles into place. This requires timing and practice, but it's a trick worth knowing. As the pieces fall faster, this gets harder to do.

You can press F3 to suspend the game and look around to see what to do, without affecting your score for that piece. Press F3 again when you're ready to move the piece.

Sneakier tricks. TETRIS is far too good a game to be lacking really sneaky tricks. Here are some of the neat things that the online help doesn't tell you how to do.

Slam dunking. Because you get more points the fewer times you move a piece, Dave Edson added a feature that lets you slam a piece down to the corners from the middle of the board with a single keystroke. You need to do a little setting up for this:

1. Quit Windows.
2. At the DOS prompt, switch to the directory in which you installed TETRIS. For example, if this is \WEP, type "cd \wep" and press Enter.
3. At the DOS prompt, type "copy con: slam.doc" and press Enter.
4. Type "This is a TETRIS file" and press F6. (It doesn't really matter what you type, as long as you press F6 afterwards.)

The next time you start TETRIS, the program notices the SLAM.DOC file in the same directory as the TETRIS.EXE file. You can now press the 1 key on the numeric pad to slam a piece to the left corner, and the 3 key to slam a piece to the right corner. Slamming can save you as many as six keystrokes and two rows of height per piece, thereby doubling or even tripling your normal score. Slamming does not work evenly for the two-player version. The player on the right can slam pieces, but the player on the left can only slam pieces to the left with the N key.

Fake out your opponent. One sneaky way to win a two-player game is to build up a lead of a few hundred points and then deliberately stack pieces up to end the game. This preempts your opponent, and you win.

Custom backgrounds. Finally, for those who are a little more technically inclined, you can tweak the TETRIS.INI file to load custom bitmaps as the background rather than using the default backgrounds that TETRIS displays. To do this, you need to edit TETRIS.INI with a sector editor such as the one in the Norton Utilities. For each of the nine levels in the game, you need to tell TETRIS to use a custom bitmap rather than the default. You also need to tell it what bitmap to use. Custom bitmaps can have a maximum of 16 colors. Before you edit TETRIS.INI, be sure to make a back-up copy of the file in case you make a mistake.

In the sector editor, look at byte 14, which controls the pattern for skill level 1. This byte can have any of the following values:

Value	What it does
00	Displays a solid color
01	Displays the default pattern (this is the default)
02	Displays a centered custom bitmap
03	Displays a tiled custom bitmap

Change the byte to 02 or 03. TETRIS now knows that it should display a custom bitmap, either centered or tiled, as the background for skill level 1. Change the corresponding even bytes starting with byte 16 for skill levels 2 through 9.

Once you tell TETRIS to use custom bitmaps, you need to tell it where to find them. Starting at byte 34 in the file, you see <none> repeated 10 times in the file. Type the fully qualified path name, starting at the left angle bracket of <none>, for each level on which you want to display a custom bitmap. For example, if you wanted to use the standard Windows bitmap, RIBBONS.BMP, you would enter C:\WINDOWS\RIBBONS.BMP.

You have up to sixty-four characters for the path and filename. The last character must be a null; that is, it must have a value of 00. When you've made your changes to TETRIS.INI, save the file, start Windows, and start TETRIS. You can quickly check the background for each level by using the Starting Level option on the Skill menu.

Although editing the TETRIS.INI file works, it's a nuisance. However, if you use Microsoft Visual BASIC and are using a 386 or better, you can make this process go more quickly. When the original version of TETRIS was created, an option to install custom bitmaps was nixed at the last minute. Dave Edson removed the menu option that allowed you to change the bitmaps, but he chose to retain the code that did the work. Dave figured that if you didn't have a way to choose the custom bitmap option from the menu, it was as good as gone. Here's how you can wake the feature up again.

Use the Microsoft Visual BASIC SENDKEY function to post the value 131 to TETRIS. This tells TETRIS to display the bitmap menu. Enter the bitmaps you want in the fields and click on OK. Now you're ready to rock'n' roll.

If you subscribe to CompuServe, there's an easier way to wake up the bitmap menu. Dave Edson has uploaded a

How many colors?   Custom bitmaps can have a maximum of 16 colors. You can't use 256-color bitmaps like CHESS.BMP.

program, TETHACK.ZIP, that turns on the bitmap menus for you. You can probably find it in the Games section. Download it, unzip it, and try it out.

No cheating allowed. Despite its fairly sophisticated hidden features, TETRIS doesn't give you any way to cheat. You still have to be good at the game to build up a really mondo score.

TicTactics

icTactics is a multi-dimensional version of Tic-Tac-Toe. You'll recognize the game you played as a kid in the three-by-three version, but TicTactics offers two additional options: three-by-three-by-three and four-by-four-by-four. If you've played Parker Brothers' Qubic, you're already familiar with the four-level pattern.

Let's face it, there just isn't much to say about Tic-Tac-Toe. It was originally called "Naughts and Crosses" or "X's and O's." You can play the three-by-three version with paper and pencil any time you're stuck in a waiting room with a five-year-old.

Object of the Game

TicTactics is another of the several games that pit your wits against the computer's. To win, you have to complete a row by lining up your little blue marbles vertically, horizontally, or diagonally before the machine gets its little red marbles lined up. You and the box take turns.

Game Window

In the default version, TicTactics opens onto a three-by-three grid. If you have a color monitor, you play the blue marbles and the computer plays the red. If you have a monochrome monitor, you play the patterned marbles and the computer plays the solid ones. Use Color on the Options menu to toggle color on if you have a color monitor

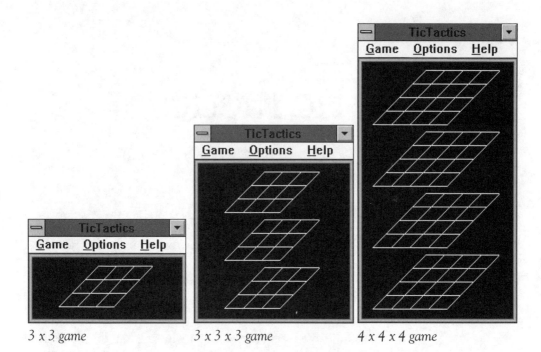

3 x 3 game   3 x 3 x 3 game   4 x 4 x 4 game

and off if you have a monochrome monitor. A check mark
appears next to the Color option when it's turned on.

Play!

Starting the game. Double-click on the TicTactics icon in
the Entertainment Pack group window. The three-by-three
grid appears, with a red marble already placed somewhere
on the grid. The game's ready to play; you don't have to
start it up.

Moves. The game proceeds with you and the computer
taking turns putting your marbles, one at a time, somewhere

From the keyboard	There are only a few things you can do with the keyboard in TicTactics. F2 starts a new game, F1 gets Help, and Esc saves pieces of your hide if the boss walks by. Other than that, you can't really play TicTactics with the keyboard. You need a mouse to place your marbles.

on the grid. You place a blue marble by clicking on an empty square. The computer responds by occupying another square. Continue placing your marbles until you or the machine fill a row or stalemate the game. The winning row flashes on the screen.

Skill levels and options. Choose Skill Level from the Options menu to tell the computer how well to play the game. TicTactics has three skill levels: Beginner, Intermediate, and Expert. At the Beginner level, the computer places marbles randomly and doesn't try to block your moves. Play at this level to learn what makes a winning row.

When you're comfortable with the Beginner skill level, switch to Intermediate. Watch the computer to learn strategy. While it still doesn't try to block you, the computer doesn't just randomly place marbles. You can see its strategy as it tries to get four in a row.

When playing the four-level board at the Master level, it's important to pay attention. That may seem obvious, but there are so many possible combinations, it's very easy to overlook the computer's strategy as you develop your own.

Use the Options menu to determine who starts first. Pick one of the options: Random player starts, Red always starts, or Blue always starts.

Choose a board layout from the Game menu.

Endgame. When you finish a game, you can start a new game by clicking the right mouse button. You can start a new game at *any* time by choosing New from the Game menu or by pressing F2.

To quit TicTactics, choose Exit from the Game menu or double-click the top-left corner of the game window.

Scoring and Winning

TicTactics is a win/lose game—no score, no best times. The winning line of marbles just lights up and flashes.

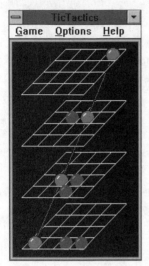

Keep your eye on the diagonals.

Shaded gray square shown here are the key squares in the 4 x 4 x 4

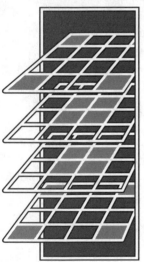

Tips, Traps, and Sneaky Tricks

If you're under the age of eight, you may be able to get more than thirty seconds out of the three-by-three layout of TicTactics before the symptoms of terminal boredom set in—but even that's doubtful

At first, the three-level layout seems to offer more challenge, but once you realize that the center square of the middle layer serves the same function as the center square of the three-by-three game, you're not going to spend much time with that variation either. Once you've captured that square, careful play will prevent your losing a game. The worst you should face is a draw.

But when you get to the four-level layout—now you've got a game! If you're new to multi-dimensional Tic-Tac-Toe, start with the Beginner skill level to learn how to lay out your marbles. Any four marbles is a winning row, but that can be hard to see at first. For instance, if you start in the middle of a row on the bottom tier and move up and diagonally, it takes a little practice to see where those marbles in the middle rows are going to go.

Although TicTactics has no Undo option on its menus, you can back up through any number of moves by clicking the right mouse button. At the end of a game, clicking the right mouse button starts a new game.

Key squares. In the four-level layout, the key squares are the corners on the top and bottom layers and the four inner squares on the two middle layers. Any of these squares can be a part of seven different combinations of four in a row. The other squares can be a part of no more than four combinations. As in any board pattern, the split is your most advantageous move. In other words, try to place your marble so that it helps create two different rows of four.

Part 3

The Microsoft Entertainment Pack: Volume Two

Because of the success of the first Microsoft Entertainment Pack, Microsoft released two more volumes of games in the fall of 1991. The Microsoft Entertainment Pack: Volume Two contains these games:

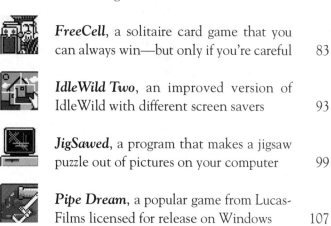

| more... | ⬇ |

CHAPTER 11

FreeCell

 nlike all the solitaire games you've seen so far, FreeCell doesn't rely on luck at all. The computer deals all the cards face up (no hidden cards)—you have to figure out how to move them around.

Jim Horne, who wrote the Windows version of FreeCell, says, "It's a great game because it seems to have some built-in psychology. When you first start, the games can be tricky, but as you get better, you find yourself winning more consistently. Soon you begin to get cocky, your concentration level drops, and bingo! you lose again. It's nice relaxation, but if you relax just a little too much, you get stuck."

By the way, FreeCell is terrific for people who spend a lot of time waiting around in airports. You can play it on a laptop without a mouse or a trackball. It has so many different deals (they seem random, but they're not) that you can play for hours without getting bored.

Object of the Game

To win FreeCell you have to move all the cards from the eight columns of the tableau to the four home cells in the upper-right corner of the window. The home cells are for suit stacks: you have to stack the cards in the home cells in ascending numerical order, by suit, aces first. To do this, you have to rearrange the random columns into numerical order, highest card at the top, and by alternating color (as you do in the Windows version of Solitaire).

Winning a game is a test of self-restraint and forethought, because the obvious moves can get you into deep trouble by blocking moves you really need to make.

Game Window

At the top of the window are two groups of four empty outlines, called *cells*. The four cells on the left are the *free cells*; the four on the right are *home cells*, where you build the suit stacks, beginning with aces. Each free cell can hold only one card at a time. They give you room to maneuver the cards in the columns. At the top center of the window is a playing-card king. Watch him as you move cards around. See if you can figure out what he's doing and why.

When you start a game, the computer deals all the cards in a standard playing deck into eight columns on the lower two-thirds of the playing area. The cells at the top stay empty until you put something in them. The title bar at the top of the window tells you the number of the game (or hand, if you prefer) that the computer just dealt you.

The Game menu lets you start a new game, restart a current game, or choose a favorite game (hand) by number. The Options menu lets you see how many games you've won and lost lately and lets you turn the messages feature on or off. FreeCell doesn't have skill levels, probably because it doesn't need them—it has 32,000 different hands to choose from.

Are all FreeCell's games really winnable?

Some of Jim Horne's ex-colleagues at the University of Alberta tested this, and they claim that all the games can be solved. The games that were too tough, they gave to their hard-core FreeCell guru, Harold. Harold can usually crack any FreeCell game in fifteen minutes. At last report, all the games were winnable. If you find one that isn't, and you can prove it, Microsoft wants to hear from you. Send your proof to Microsoft Entertainment Pack Manager, One Microsoft Way, Redmond, WA, 98037-9717.

FreeCell starting layout

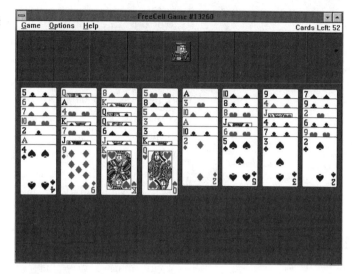

Play!

Starting a game. Choose FreeCell from the Entertainment Pack Two group window by double-clicking on the king icon. When the game starts, the play area is bare except for the outlines of the cells at the top of the window. Start a new game by clicking New game under the Game menu, or by pressing F2. FreeCell deals a hand. Although the cards overlap, you can tell what most of them are, except for the suit of the aces.

Your first response to the initial deal might be "@#$&%?!!!" or "How am I going to get those three aces off the back row?" Just remember—all the games, in theory, are winnable.

Moves. You play FreeCell by shifting the cards around the play area, creating runs in the columns and then moving them to the suit stacks. The way you move the cards depends on where you're moving them to and from. Watch out! FreeCell has no undo command. Once you move, you're committed: "A card laid is a card played." If you mess up, you have to play on or restart the game.

FreeCell gives you six legal ways to move the cards around the game window. Here they are:

Column to column. You can play the bottom card on one column to the bottom card of another only if the target card is the opposite color and one rank higher. For example, you can play the deuce of clubs on the three of diamonds.

Click on the card you want to move; it changes to inverse video. Then click anywhere on the column you want to move the card to. If you try to make an illegal move, FreeCell tells you that you can't do it. If you change your mind about moving a card, just click on the card again. Be careful with your clicking. If you accidentally double-click (that is, click twice in succession, very fast), the card flips off the column to an empty free cell, if there is one. If you change your mind, change it slowly.

Don't make a move just because you can. Think ahead. Will the move uncover another card you really need? An ace maybe? When you uncover an ace in one of the columns, it floats gracefully on its own to the next available home cell at the top-right corner of the window.

Column to free cell. The free cells are free because you can put anything you want in them. Any card is a legal move, as long as a free cell is empty. Do not abuse the privilege, however. Make this move only when it gives you the advantage of more moves. For example, suppose

Aces

When the computer deals a hand with an ace at the bottom of one of the columns, the ace doesn't go anywhere until you click on it. Then it floats up to a home cell. If more than one ace is exposed at the deal (you lucky dog), click twice on any card to start the aces moving to the home cells. If the appropriate deuces are exposed, they also begin their journey to the home cells on their own.

You can see the suit of a partially hidden ace by putting the cursor on the card and holding down the right mouse button. For those of you without a mouse, type the number of the column (from 1 to 8), then type it again. FreeCell slowly displays all the cards in the column.

column two has an exposed black king at the bottom. Column four's bottom four cards are a red ten, a black jack, a red queen, and a red ace. Move the ten, jack, and queen to three empty free cells, which exposes the ace. The ace automatically floats up to a home cell. Then play the queen, jack, and ten on the king, which frees the free cells for more maneuvering.

Double-click on the card you want to move to a free cell. The card flips off the column and floats to the first available empty free cell, if there is one. If all the free cells are occupied already, double-clicking has no effect.

Watch out! Once you play a card on a free cell, you can't move it back to a column except to a card that's one rank higher and of the opposite color, or to an empty column.

Free cell to column. It's a good idea to clear out your free cells as soon as you can, to make room for more maneuvering. The column-to-column rule applies here: the card you want to move has to be one rank lower than the destination card, and of the opposite color. So, for example, you can play a black jack on an exposed red queen. Click on the card you want to move, then click anywhere on the destination column.

Free cell to home cell. Move cards to the home cells judiciously—that's how you win. To move a card to a home cell from a free cell (or from a column, for that matter) the exposed card in the free cell has to be the same suit and one

Speed tip

You can move a run of up to five cards at once from one column to the bottom card of another column, as long as you have enough free cells to hold the run you want to move. Click on the bottom card of the run you want move. Then click on the bottom card of the destination column. All the cards in the run zip first to the free cells, then automatically to the destination column. If you have an empty column, you can move twice as many cards by splitting a column and moving it in two moves.

rank lower than the card you want to play. Home cell stacks start with an ace and go in ascending numerical order. For instance, you can play a deuce of clubs on an ace of clubs, a three of clubs on the deuce, and so on.

Click on the card you want to move, then click on the home cell. Beware! Once you put a card on a home cell stack, you can't take it back!

Column to home cell. Click on the card you want to move, then click on the home cell. The rules for free cell to home cell apply to this kind of move as well. The home cell you want to move to has to show a card of the same suit and one rank lower than the card you want to move.

Empty columns. An empty column is even better than an empty free cell, because you can put more than one card there! You can move any free card to an empty column. A good strategy is to open up one or more empty columns as you rearrange the cards. Then you can start a new column with any card, from another column or from a free cell. Once you start a new column, it's just like any other column: you can only play cards one rank lower and of the opposite color. So don't start a new column with a deuce.

Automatic moves. At the end of each move, FreeCell automatically moves all the legal exposed cards to the home-cell stacks, if they're not playable elsewhere. In other words, the game plays a qualified card automatically on a home cell if there are no lower-ranked cards of the opposite color anywhere in the columns on the main playing area.

Endgame. The game ends when you get all the cards into the home cells, or (more often) when all your moves are blocked and there's nowhere else you can go. If you lose, FreeCell prompts you to play the same game again.

If you win, the last few cards are especially fun to move, because the computer takes over and moves whole stacks of cards from the columns to the home-cell stacks. You've found the key to the puzzle when you make a move and suddenly your screen goes wild with flying cards.

Play again. You can try the same game again by choosing Restart game from the Game menu, even when a game is in progress. To play a different game, choose New game from the Game menu, or press F2. If you do this before you finish your current game, FreeCell asks you if you're ready to resign. Click on OK to start the new game.

If you're really compulsive and keep track of the numbers of your favorite games, choose Select game from the

From the keyboard

You don't need a mouse to play Freecell, but it's a lot easier if you have one. To play Freecell from the keyboard, you have to remember a few numeric codes for various locations on the play area. The columns on the tableau are 1 to 8, counting from left to right. All the home cells are 9. The free cells are 10.

To move a card from one column to another, type the column number of the card you want to move, followed by the destination column number. The card flips neatly to its target. If you want to move a card from a column to a free cell, type the number of the column, then type a 10. The card flips to the first empty free cell. To move a card from a free cell to a column or a home cell, type a zero repeatedly until the card you want is highlighted; then type the code for its destination (1 through 9). For instance if you want to move a deuce of clubs from the second free cell to a home cell that has the ace of clubs on it, type a zero twice, then type a 9. If you want to send it to a three of hearts on the fourth column, type the zero twice, then type a 4. Finally, to send any card to a home cell, type the number of the column, then type a 9. If the card's legal, it knows which free cell to go to.

To start a new game at random, press F2. If you want to select a specific game, press F3 and then type the number of the game. Press F4 to see your statistics. To get Help, press F1. Press Esc to shrink the screen to an icon if the boss appears suddenly.

Game menu. Type the number of your chosen game in the dialog box, and click on OK.

To quit the game, choose Exit from the Game menu and take the loss in the game statistics. Alternatively, double-click on the top-left button on the game window, or quit Windows entirely.

Scoring and Winning

FreeCell is a simple win/lose proposition. There's no numerical score, and going fast doesn't get you anything. You win if you manage to get all the cards in the deck up to the home cells. If you can't, you lose. The game keeps track of your wins and losses by number and by percentage of total games played. To check your current win/loss totals, choose Statistics from the Options menu or press F4.

Tips, Traps, and Sneaky Tricks

The surest way to win is to look at FreeCell as a puzzle. A puzzle requires patience and careful consideration of each move; so does FreeCell. Think ahead. It's all too easy to move the cards around, making runs, just to realize that you've completely blocked yourself.

Don't make long runs of cards (more than four) in the lower columns if there are cards above them that don't belong in the run. Eventually, you'll have to find a place to park that long run in order to free the other cards. Unless you've freed up several empty columns, you may find yourself fatally stuck.

Empty columns come in handy for moving cards around. Don't be too quick to fill them with a run unless you can move a lot of cards off other stacks into the new stack. Alternatively, use empty columns as you would the free cells; they make good temporary holding places for inconvenient cards.

If you get tired of listening to FreeCell tell you what is and isn't a legal move, go to the Options menu and choose Messages. When there is no checkmark beside this option,

FreeCell minds its own business (although you still can't make an illegal move).

When you move a card, it drifts leisurely across the screen and gently lands in place. This little dance will eventually drive you nuts, but there is an alternative. To play power FreeCell, press Ctrl-F2; the cards snap smartly to their places. To go back to slow mode, press Ctrl-F1.

If you get carried away with moving cards through mid-air, the title bar flashes. Yes, you're in deep trouble. Maybe. That's your warning that only one legal move is left. Sometimes this legal move is very hard to see, although refilling your coffee cup often helps.

Beat the statistics by quitting Windows when you know you're losing anyway. When you quit Windows, FreeCell doesn't record it as a loss in its cumulative win/loss tally, because you're still trying to win it. FreeCell records a loss if you quit the program with a game in progress, if you resign by starting a new game, and, of course, if you lose a game. You can replay the same game immediately without affecting your score—trying a game half a dozen times before you win counts as one win and one loss. If your score starts to show too many losses, you can clear the statistics and start over by clicking on the Clear button at the bottom of the FreeCell Statistics dialog box, under the Options menu.

You can see what happens when you win by pressing Ctrl-Shift-F10 at any time during a game. When the "User-Friendly User Interface" dialog box appears, choose Abort. The dialog box disappears. On your next move, FreeCell starts moving cards to home stacks in no particular order and shows you what it looks like when you win a game.

Oh, by the way, remember that king icon at the top of the playing field? Notice how he turns his head back and forth when you make a move? It doesn't mean anything. Jim Horne just thought it was cool, so he put it in.

CHAPTER 13

IdleWild Two

dleWild is included with all three Microsoft Entertainment Packs. It isn't really a game, but a program for running a set of screen savers when your Windows applications are on idle for a while.

Brad Christian developed the first version of IdleWild as an exercise in writing OS/2 Presentation Manager applications. He then rewrote it for Windows. Brad, along with Tony Krueger, also wrote the eight screen animations that went with the program. This version of IdleWild was included in the first Microsoft Entertainment Pack.

A number of other screen savers were floating around Microsoft when the Entertainment Packs Two and Three were under development. Some were enhancements of public domain programs, and many were the original creations of Microsoft developers and programmers. Microsoft included the hottest of these in Volumes Two and Three.

The IdleWild program is similar in all three volumes of the Entertainment Packs. Some of the screen savers in Volumes Two and Three seem to miss the point though. The idea of a screen saver is to keep a static screen image from burning onto the screen. Although this isn't as much a problem with monitors now as it was in the past, all the screen savers in Volume One are animations that keep changing the screen image. But several of the screen savers in Volumes Two and Three just exchange one static image for another (Mandelbrot is a good example). Also, many of the screen savers in Volume One offered privacy by covering or distorting the screen image when you aren't using the computer. Again, some of the screen saver modules in Volumes Two and Three don't do that. They return to the original screen image when they're finished running.

Despite these limitations, Volumes Two and Three offer a few great new options in response to users' comments about Volume One. The most complained about feature of IdleWild One is that it's too easy to blank the screen accidentally when moving the cursor to the upper-right corner to minimize a window or activate the help menu. With the new Hot Corners option included with Volumes Two and Three, you can decide which corner blanks the screen and which corner disables IdleWild temporarily.

The most requested new feature that Microsoft added for Volumes Two and Three is a user-defined password or set of keystrokes, without which no one can reactivate the screen. This offers privacy that can't be invaded by a random keystroke or mouse movement. Volumes Two and Three contain the option that lets you create a password if you want one.

Each volume of the Entertainment Packs contains a different set of animations. The setup procedure included with the Entertainment Packs automatically copies everything to the WEP directory. This gives each volume access to all of the screen savers, not just the ones included with that volume. If possible, install Volume Two or Three after you install Volume One, to ensure that you have the broadest set of options for IdleWild. For information about the screen savers in Volumes One and Three, see the other IdleWild chapters in this book.

Running IdleWild

To start IdleWild, double-click on the IdleWild icon in the Entertainment Pack Two group window. The IdleWild window appears, in two sections. The section on the left lists the names of the available screen savers. A bar on the side lets you scroll to the screen savers that aren't currently visible. The section on the right lists information about the highlighted screen saver. IdleWild has two drop-down menus: Options and Help. (Any menu item is active when a checkmark is next to it.)

IdleWild Two
opening window

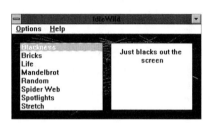

Many of the options included with IdleWild Two and Three are exactly the same as Volume One. For information about how to use Set Delay, Blank Pointer, Autoload, Blank Now, and Exit, see the chapter on IdleWild, page 43. The additional options are Module, Password, and Hot Corners.

Module offers you a set of run options for some of the IdleWild Two screen savers, to customize how the screen saver will run on your machine. See the descriptions of the screen savers on page 97for more about the module options that go with the screen saver you're interested in. IdleWild Two has three screen savers that come with options: Spider, Spotlights, and Stretch. Press F2 when one of these savers is highlighted on the list in the IdleWild window. An Options box appears. Set the options from this box.

Password lets you set a password. Once you set a password, it has to be typed in before Windows will leave IdleWild and restore the current application to your screen. Click on Password to bring up the password dialog box.

Use caution when you set this option, so you don't find you've shut yourself out of your own workstation. For the best results, follow these steps:

Password dialog box

1. Make sure there's no "X" in the small box in the lower-left corner next to "Disable Password Protection." If there is, click on the X to turn on Password Protection.
2. Click in the box following "New Password." Type a password, preferably something terribly witty that no one would associate with you. Click in the "Confirm Password" box and retype the password.
3. Click on the OK button or press Enter.

From now on, when IdleWild has control of the screen it demands the password before it relinquishes control of the screen and restores the current application.

To change your password, choose Password from the Options menu. A dialog box appears, asking you for your old password. Type it in. Click in the New password box and type in the new password. Click in Confirm Password box and retype the new password. Click on the OK button or press Enter. You're ready to rock 'n' roll.

To disable password protection, choose Password from the Options menu. Enter your password in the dialog box. Click in the box next to Disable Password Protection and click on the OK button or press Enter. Now absolutely anyone can see your screen.

Hot Corners lets you tell the program which corner will blank the screen immediately when you put the pointer there. It also lets you decide which corner will temporarily disable IdleWild. In the Microsoft Entertainment Pack, Volume One, you instantly blank the screen by moving your cursor to the upper-right corner or temporarily disable IdleWild by moving it to the lower-right corner of the screen. In Volume Two, you can choose your own corners for these two functions.

Hot Corners dialog box

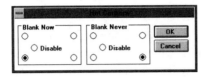

To pick a corner, choose Hot Corners on the Options menu. In the Blank Now half of the box, click the dot in the position of the corner you want to use for instant blanking. The best corner to pick for blanking the screen instantly is the lower-left because you don't go down to that corner of the screen too often so you won't be likely to blank the screen by accident.

The Blank Never portion of the Hot Corners box lets you temporarily disable the screen blanker. To pick a corner as the Blank Never option, choose Hot Corners from the Options menu. Click the dot in the position of the corner you want to use to temporarily disable blanking. Press Enter or click OK to continue.

Volume Two Screen Savers

The IdleWild feature in Microsoft Entertainment Pack, Volume Two, gives you a choice of eight different screen saver schemes. Here's what each does:

Blackness wipes everything from the screen and displays the same black screen you have when your machine is off.

Bricks divides the screen into one of several different sizes of grids. Bricks dissolve one at a time, and the column above the emptied square falls to fill the space.

Life is a life simulation similar to LifeGenesis (a game included with Microsoft Entertainment Pack, Volume Three). The screen fills with a bunch of colored squares, which are supposed to represent living, breeding cells that are born, reproduce, and die before your eyes. If you find this interesting, you may want to turn to the chapter of this

	book that describes LifeGenesis for a more detailed explanation of life simulations.
Mandelbrot	generates a Mandelbrot fractal. The Mandelbrot set is a curve mathematically described by a formula that a man named Mandelbrot discovered and popularized. The picture you get is the edge of the curve.
Random	selects and runs a screen saver at random.
Spider Web	has an invisible spider spinning webs across your screen. The web begins with lines that look like an asterisk. Then the spider spins round and round in a spiral until it completes the web. After a few seconds the web disappears and the spider begins again.

You can pick the skill level of the spider from the Module Options box under the Options menu, or by pressing F2. The webs the spider weaves are more complex as you progress from the Rookie to the Professional level. The Random option picks a spider skill level for you.

Spotlights   darkens your screen image and shines spotlights across it.

You can determine how dark your screen gets before the spotlight start by setting the Spotlight Options box. Press F2 to bring up the Options box. Click the dot next to Light, Medium, Dark, Black, or Random to make your selection. Then click the dot next to the shape you want the spotlights to be: Circle or Square. Slide the button on the scroll bar to choose the number of spotlights, from one to four. Slide the button on the lower scroll bar to adjust size. When you're done, click OK or press Enter.

Stretch   zooms in on your screen, flips it upside down and zooms back out. When you press F2, you can choose whether to use an intermediate memory bitmap. If you don't use one, IdleWild stretches the screen a section at a time. If you do, IdleWild stretches the screen in memory and then displays the whole thing at once. Stretching looks better done that way. However, this also takes a lot more memory. If you don't have enough, Windows uses its swapfile, which can really slow the process down. Try both styles out and see which you prefer.

CHAPTER 12

JigSawed

 igSawed is a computer version of the good old-fashioned jigsaw puzzle. It's a little different from the kind that comes in pieces in a box, but if you like working puzzles you'll be glad you made the effort to adjust. Some of the differences are even advantages: the puzzles are smaller than most manual jigsaw puzzles, so you can work them in a few minutes. Better still, the pieces never get lost.

Tito Messerli created JigSawed to see what it was like to write a very graphic program in Microsoft Visual Basic. When the call went out for games for Volumes Two and Three of the Microsoft Entertainment Packs, Tito polished JigSawed and added a few features.

Object of the Game

The idea here is to put the puzzle together as fast as possible.

Game Window

The JigSawed window is like an empty card table waiting for you to dump out your puzzle pieces. Around the right and bottom edges are vertical and horizontal scroll bars that let you see the edges of the puzzle. In the lower-right corner of the window is a timer. Across the top of the window is the title bar, where the name of the picture file you're working on appears.

In the top-left corner are the menu names. On the Game menu, you find Open, Paste, Scramble, Solve, Fast

Solve, Hint, and Exit. On the Options menu are Maximize Workspace, Fast Move, Show Scrambling, Scramble on Open, Timer, Sound, Show hidden pieces, Background, Outline, and Shape. If an option is active, a checkmark appears next to its name in the Options menu.

When you open one of the five picture-puzzle files that come with the game, the computer dumps the puzzle pieces into the window. It's a bit nicer than dumping real puzzle pieces out of a box, because the pieces here all land face-up in the right direction, although some pieces may cover some others.

Play!

Starting the game. Start JigSawed by double-clicking the JigSawed icon in the Entertainment Pack Two group window. It opens to the About JigSawed box. Click on OK or press Enter to continue.

Choose Open from the Game menu and pick the puzzle you want from the list box that appears. The list box displays the filenames of the available pictures. Pick one with a .BMP extension. You can double-click on the filename in the list box, or click on the filename and then click on OK (or press Enter).

A frame appears in the game window. In a second or so, the scrambled pieces of the picture appear. If you don't know exactly how the picture should look when it's put together, choose Fast Solve from the Game menu. In a few seconds the pieces resolve themselves into a coherent

Get your kids to play JigSawed

Almost all kids love jigsaw puzzles. JigSawed gives them an opportunity to play a computer game without the pressure of enemies pursuing them or beeps and bells to distract them. They work at their own speed. They learn and practice several complex mouse operations, such as dragging the puzzle pieces, while learning about spatial relations. Best of all, they have FUN!

TANKER.BMP all
scrambled up

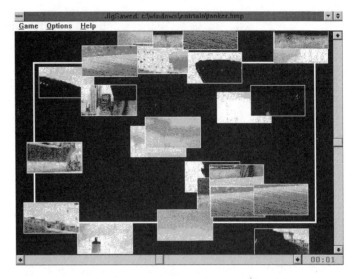

whole. Study the picture, then choose Scramble from the
Game menu to rescramble the image.

Setting the options. When you start JigSawed for the first
time, several of the options are set to default values. The
pieces of the puzzle are rectangle-shaped, the background
is black, and the outline is white. Sometimes these default
options are fine, but sometimes they can make it hard to
see the puzzle clearly.

TANKER.BMP solved

Change any options that don't work for the picture you've chosen. If you need a different-colored background, choose Background from the Options menu. A box appears that lets you pick something other than black. Click on a color that's different from the color of most of your puzzle pieces and then click on OK.

The Shape extended menu gives you a choice of different shapes for the puzzle piece: rectangles, circles, ellipses, stars, or ellipses in rectangles. If you have a slower machine, don't choose the non-rectangular pieces, because it takes a lot more time to move them.

In the same way, the extended Outline menu gives you a choice of outlines: black, white, or none.

If you don't want to work against the clock, you can turn off the timer by choosing Timer from the Options menu. When it's off, the check mark disappears.

You can also turn the sound off, by choosing Sound from the Options menu. But doing this may put you into a bind: if some puzzle pieces look exactly the same (say, solid-color pieces that are the same shape), the only way you can tell if they're in the right place is that the computer beeps to let you know you got it right. Leave the sound on.

Moves. Start just as you would with a regular jigsaw puzzle by finding the corners and putting them in place. To pick up a puzzle piece and move it, just drag the piece to the position you want to try. If you've gotten it right, the computer beeps when you take your finger off the mouse button. You don't have to position the piece exactly: if you get it mostly over the hole, the piece snaps into place.

Endgame. When you finish a puzzle, the computer says, "You have solved the puzzle in x minutes and y seconds." X and y are the number of minutes and seconds it took you to solve the puzzle. Click on OK or press Enter to continue.

You can't lose at this game, but you can give up (or get bored). To switch to a different puzzle, choose Open from the Game menu and pick another picture from the list. To quit JigSawed, choose Exit from the Game menu, or double-click the top-left corner of the game window.

Variations. If you get tired of working the puzzles supplied with the Microsoft Entertainment Pack, Volume Two, you can open almost any bitmapped file (any file with the extension .BMP) that's within the JigSawed size limits. The minimum size is 32 by 32 pixels; the maximum size depends on the type of monitor you have.

Choose Open from the Game menu. Double-click on the file folder next to C:\ in the Directories box. This displays a list of directories. Double-click on the file folder next to the name of the directory that contains the file you want to turn into a puzzle. A list of files that JigSawed can open appears in the Files box. Double-click on the name of the file you want to open.

From the keyboard

You can't use the keyboard to move the puzzle pieces, but you can improve your playing time by using the keyboard shortcuts for commands. This is especially useful if you've expanded the game window to fill the screen, since this hides the menus.

Pressing Ctrl-W, or right-clicking in the work space, toggles back and forth between the expanded game window and the regular window with menus and borders.

Here are some more keyboard shortcuts:

Ctrl-D	shows hidden pieces
Ctrl-T	toggles the timer on and off
Ctrl-O	brings up the box that lets you choose a picture
Shift-Ins	pastes a picture from the clipboard
Ctrl-S	scrambles the puzzle pieces
Ctrl-V	toggles between Solve and Stop solving
Ctrl-H	gives you a hint
Ctrl-F	solves the puzzle instantly
Alt-F4	quits JigSawed

If the image is too big or has too many colors for JigSawed, the game tells you what the acceptable image sizes are. Click on OK and choose another file from the list. If the image is the right size, the computer dumps it into the frame in scrambled pieces, and you can begin.

Besides the bitmaps that come with JigSawed, you can use most of the wallpaper bitmaps that come with Windows. (Unfortunately, JigSawed won't let you use 256-color bitmaps such as CHESS.BMP.) Windows Paintbrush can save files as bitmaps. You can also get bitmaps from bulletin boards, online information services, shareware distributors, and user groups. Bitmaps of 640×480 pixels are the best ones to use with a VGA monitor.

You're supposed to be able to use most files with the extensions .BMP, .DIB, .WMF, or .ICO with JigSawed. Unfortunately, files with the extension .ICO (icon files) are too small to solve. JigSawed will also open metafiles used by programs like Windows PowerPoint. If you're making new puzzles for yourself, check your Windows applications to see what graphics formats they can read and save.

When you find files that make good puzzles, you can get to them faster if you copy them to the \WEP directory. That puts their names in the Files box automatically when you choose Open from the Game menu. (If you're going to do this, be sure to copy the files; don't simply move them. If you move them, other programs that use them may not be able to find them.)

Scoring and Winning

There isn't any scoring in JigSawed, but the timer is running, so work fast! Even though JigSawed doesn't keep

Bypassing the About JigSawed box

You can bypass the About JigSawed box that comes up every time you open the game by pressing Enter as soon as the JigSawed window appears. Wait a second or two, then click on the Game menu.

TREE.BMP solved

track of best times, as some of the other games do, you'll develop a sense of what's fast and what isn't. You'll want to work to beat your best.

Tips, Traps, and Sneaky Tricks

If you want JigSawed to give you a head start, choose Solve from the Game menu (or press Ctrl-V). Let the computer work on the puzzle until it's at a place where you want to take over. Choose Stop Solving from the Game menu (or press Ctrl-V again) and finish the puzzle yourself.

If you just want to see how the pieces fit together before you solve the puzzle, try this trick. First, choose Fast Solve from the Game menu, to put the picture together. Then click Outline on the Options menu and change the outline to White. Even if the white outline option is already on, the outline of the pieces shows up on the solved picture. The patterns are very regular, which makes them easy to remember. Now choose Scramble (Ctrl-S) from the Game menu to rescramble the picture.

If you want to expand the game window to fill the screen, click on the work area with the right mouse button. Expanding the window doesn't make the image any bigger, but it does clear away distractions like title and scroll bars, which makes it easier to concentrate on the puzzle. You can turn the menus back on by right-clicking the mouse again. (You can do the same thing by choosing Maximize Workspace from the Options menu.)

If you just want to see one piece put into place, choose Hint from the Game menu. Getting a hint costs you, however; the game adds five seconds to your time.

If you think you know roughly where a particular piece goes, a good sneaky trick is to drop the piece where you think it should go. As soon as the piece covers up more than three-quarters of the right spot, it snaps into place.

When you're still new at this, choose the circle or ellipse shapes from the Options menu. They're the easiest to solve. This is a good way to get used to JigSawed.

While you're placing the corners, rearrange the pieces on the screen, grouping by common characteristics. If pieces seem to be lost, they're probably just hiding under other pieces. Choose Show Hidden Pieces from the Options menu, or press Ctrl-D, to bring them to the surface.

You can cut or copy a picture from some other Windows application, then switch to JigSawed and use the Paste command to load the picture into JigSawed and try it out.

CHAPTER 14

Pipe Dream

ipe Dream is a plumber's nightmare. The goo runs down the pipe, and you have to build a system to run it down the drain (or outside) before the goo gets to the end of the pipe and spills. If the goo spills, you may find some guys in moonsuits at your door ready to clean up the mess. But what about the mess on the scoreboard?

Pipe Dream (known as "Pipe Mania" in the European version) is the Windows version of the LucasFilm game of the same name. Wes Cherry, the programmer who wrote Solitaire, found the LucasFilm game during one of his "finals week at Harvey Mudd" adventures. After he went to Microsoft, he worked on implementing Pipe Dream as an exercise in Windows programming. It became so popular at Microsoft that they decided not to keep it to themselves and included it in this game package. A hearty "good job, dude" goes to Wes for delivering this slick game.

The beautiful window patterns come from the fingers of Leslie Kooy. The patterns can either help your game or make it more challenging, but they're always fun to look at.

Object of the Game

The object of Pipe Dream is to build a plumbing system from pieces of pipe to run the goo from its source to a safe place—and keep the goo flowing long enough to satisfy a time limit. In doing so, you rack up mega-points and dazzle your friends (and yourself) with your totally awesome score.

Game Window

The Pipe Dream window is dominated by a gray three-dimensional grid with the Pipe Dream title in the center. The pointer in this one is especially nice—it's a three-dimensional pipe wrench.

The playing area is surrounded by a red border. On the left side of the window, there's a vertical column that has some funny-shaped black lines on a gray background. These are some of the spare pipes you'll use to build your plumbing system. There are eight basic pipes:

Pieces of pipe

The Start piece (shown at the left in this picture) appears as the first piece on each gameboard. An inexhaustible supply of goo flows from the Start piece. The next half-dozen pieces are easy to understand: goo flows in one end and out the other. The eighth piece in the group is called a crossover. You can use this piece to make loops in the pipe, such as the one shown in the next picture.

Goo always flows in a straight line unless something changes its direction. When you build a loop, the goo flows through it in one direction, then doubles back and flows through the other direction. Goo won't hang a right turn at a crossover, though; you have to use a curved piece of pipe or build a loop to change the goo's flow direction.

Pipe Dream graphics	Like many of the games in the Microsoft Entertainment Packs, the graphics are much better on a color VGA monitor. You simply can't see the fancy graphics on an EGA monitor. Get yourself a color VGA monitor to play Pipe Dream.

A loop with goo running through it

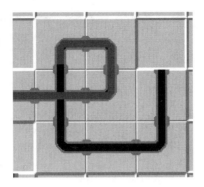

Now take a look at the rest of the window. Directly below the spare pipes are two little buttons. The button on the left has a double arrow pointing off to the right. That's the fast flow button, which speeds up the flow of goo through your plumbing system, giving you a higher score. To the right of the flow button is a button with a question mark. That's the shortcut to the Help files.

Continuing around the window you see the Pipe Dream icon at the top of the spare pipe bin. Directly above the icon is a (skill) Level box. As you play through the levels the number in the box helps you keep track of where you are. Beside the Level box is the Score box. The number in the box changes as you play and earn points.

To the right of the Score box is a string of indicators side-by-side in a long bar. That bar is the gauge for the minimum length of your plumbing system. As the goo runs through each piece of your plumbing system, the buttons in the gauge disappear one by one from the left side. When all the buttons have disappeared, you've satisfied the minimum distance requirement.

Play!

Starting the Game. Start Pipe Dream by double-clicking on the Pipe Dream icon in the Entertainment Pack Two group window. The game window appears and a credit screen fades in. The game begins when you click on the playing area. The credit screen disappears and a Start piece

*Starting Pipe
Dream window*

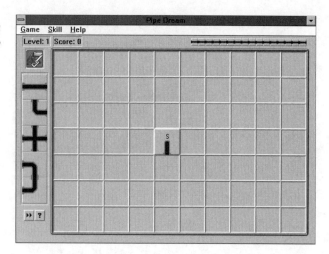

appears somewhere on the grid. The goo flows from the Start square in the direction of the opening after a *short* pause (about 10 seconds).

Moves. The first piece of pipe you have to place is the one on the bottom of the spare pipe dispenser. You place a piece of pipe by clicking the mouse (your pipe wrench) on the grid square where you want the piece to go. Pieces of pipe can't be rotated, flipped, or changed; you have to play them as they appear. You also to have play every pipe in the order it appears in the dispenser.

If you're lucky, you can plunk the piece down next to the outflow from the Start piece, giving the goo somewhere further to go. Otherwise, you need to place the piece somewhere else on the grid. The next piece in the dispenser may fit next to the goo outflow and join with the first piece.

Each time you place a piece on the grid, another piece appears at the top of spare pipe dispenser. Keep an eye on what's coming up and plan your plumbing system. Remember, you don't have to lay the pipe in the exact order the goo is going to flow through them. If you see that the pipe that's the second one up in the bin is the one that fits next to the opening and the first one will connect to that, you can click on the square where the first pipe goes. Then

*Pipe Dream game
in progress*

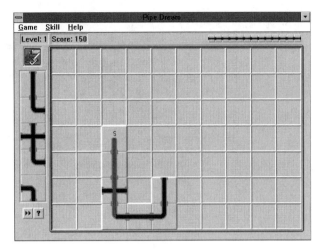

quickly click on the square next to the opening to lay the second pipe. Remember to lay the pipe in the order of the spare pipes in the dispenser—not the order that the goo will flow through them.

Take a close look at the gauge at the top-right of the window. The buttons look a little like miniature pipe pieces—and they are. You need to keep building the plumbing system until you have the goo going through at least as many squares as there are pieces in the minimum distance gauge. (As you might expect, the number of pieces in the gauge goes up with the levels.)

Skill Levels. When the goo gets to the end of the pipe, it either gushes out if the plumbing system wasn't long enough (which ends the game) or it just stops. You then see the "Click for next level" message. When you click on the message, you're at Level 2 and the goo starts flowing in ten

**Replacing
pieces of pipe**

If you put a piece in the wrong place, you can replace it with another piece by clicking on top of it. This "blows up" the first piece and replaces it with the current piece of pipe. Don't do this if you can avoid it, though! It costs you 50 points and a lot of time.

You're ready to go to the next level.

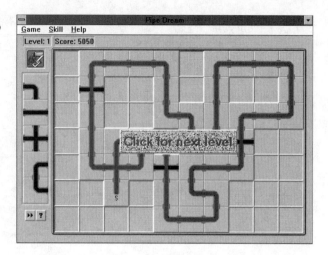

seconds. Level 2 is much like Level 1, but the goo flows quicker and you need to build a longer plumbing system.

When you get to Level 3, the border on the screen is broken in a couple of places. You can run the goo out one of the openings and it magically (and instantly) appears at the opening immediately opposite it. If you run the goo out an opening, be ready at the other side with more plumbing.

After you win at Level 4 (where more holes in the border appear), you don't see Level 5 right away. You see the first bonus level. Bonus levels are nearly full of random pipe pieces. Unlike the previous levels, you don't actually have

The goo goes out one side and comes back in on the other side.

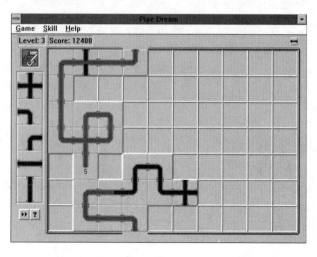

to run the goo anywhere. You can sit back and not connect a single piece and you still go to Level 5. The bonus window is where you can rack up a lot of extra points.

One of the squares in the bonus window doesn't have a piece in it. You move pieces by clicking on one of the pieces next to the empty square. That piece snaps into the empty square. You connect the pipes by moving pieces around. Try to build as long a section as you can (you get more points that way). When you complete the bonus level, a password appears. Remember it; it will let you bypass the first four levels next time you play.

Level 5 has a different pattern and a few new features. The new pattern uses some rather attractive 3-D effects. There are two new items on the board. The first is just a block with no features. Blocks are there to make your life more difficult by blocking your progress. You can't put a spare piece of pipe here; you have to construct around it. The second new feature looks rather like a python that's eaten a beach ball. This is the *reservoir* piece. The *reservoir* won't let the goo flow through it until it fills up with goo, so you get some extra time. The down side of reservoirs is you don't get to move them, remove them, or replace them with any other pieces—and sometimes they're just not in a very helpful place.

First bonus level (note the reservoir pieces)

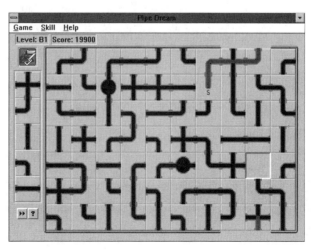

At Level 9, you first see the "bonus" pieces on the board. These look like regular pipe pieces, except that they say "Bonus." You can't move these or bomb them with another piece. You get extra points for sending goo through them. Level 9 also has "one-way" pipe pieces. These look like regular pipe pieces except that they have arrows indicating the direction in which the goo must flow. If you try to send goo through them the wrong way, it all flows out at the juncture. This feature is here just to make the game harder.

At Level 17, you see a piece on the board that looks the drain on a shower. This is an "end" piece. Up until now, you could just run the goo around and around until the gauge ran out of units, but no longer. To complete a level, you have to run the goo around the minimum distance *and* have it go out the drain! As you might imagine, this can be pretty tricky at times.

There are nine different patterns in Pipe Dream. After each four levels, you have a chance to rack up points on the bonus level and earn the password for the next level. You can actually keep going after level 36, but the patterns don't change after that.

Choosing a Skill Level. The Skill menu is really a list of the playing levels, in four level increments, from Level 1 to Level 33. Once you've gotten the hang of the lower levels of Pipe Dream, you'll probably want to skip to the higher levels and play there to go even higher. When you click on any of the levels on the Skill menu (other than Level 1), you have to supply the password for that level. Here's a hint: the password for Level 5 is "plam." You're going to have to earn the rest of them … or will you? Look in the "Tips, Traps, and Sneaky Tricks" section for a trick on how to avoid the passwords and play at any level you like.

| More FX | Wes and Leslie had a lot of fun with the 3-D effects on the various pieces. After a while, it got to be so much that Wes's code refers to it as "Gratuitous 3-D Effect!" |

Endgame. If you choose Exit from the Game menu to quit a game, your score isn't recorded in the high scores. (This may be good or bad, depending.) If you have a high score but you're just bone tired, you can always quit the game by letting the goo run out the end of a pipe. That method ends the game and records your score so you can go back later and gloat. Press F2 to start over.

Scoring and Winning

Pipe Dream is one game where you can rack up some amazingly high scores with practice and a few tricks. If you're playing the game for high scores, you may not make it to as high a level as if you're playing to see how high a level you can reach (if that makes any sense).

Scoring is based on three factors: the length of your plumbing system, the time you take to build the system, and the way you use some of the pieces. The length of the system is important for scoring, because the longer the system, the more pieces you use. You earn 50 points for each pipe the goo actually goes through. After the minimum distance gauge runs out you earn 100 points for each pipe.

Your speed in laying pipe is also important, because the sooner you're done plumbing the system, the sooner you can click on the fast flow button to speed up the goo. After you hit the fast flow button, you earn double the usual points for each pipe the goo goes through, so if you're beyond the minimum distance and you hit the flow button, you earn 200 points for each pipe.

The way you use the pipes is important to your score, too. When you use the crossover pipes and the goo actually crosses itself you earn an extra 500 points. If you run the goo through five loops in one level, you earn a 5000-point

From the keyboard

Pipe Dream depends heavily on the mouse. It lets you use only the regulation hurry-up keys: F1 for Help, F2 for a new game, F3 to pause, and Esc to save your job.

bonus. When you run the goo through a bonus or reservoir piece, you earn 500 points for each piece. As before, you get double points if you're beyond the minimum distance. You also earn 1000 points for using the drain.

You can also have points taken away, a bit like demerits. You're penalized 50 points each time you blow up a pipe and lay a new one. But it costs you 100 points if you don't use a pipe you've laid somewhere on the board by the time you finish your system. Choices, choices . . .

If you make a really prodigious score, you can enter your name in the High Score dialog box for all to see.

Tips, Traps, and Sneaky Tricks

For high scoring, there's no better helper than the Pause key, F3, which lets you look over the board while stopping the flow of goo. Pause the game, plan your move, click to place the spare piece, and press F3 again. If you're quick with F3, the goo hardly moves enough to worry about. Playing with F3 lets you build long and complicated plumbing systems (using all the reservoirs, bonus pieces, and cross-overs) without time pressure. If you're very fast using F3, you'll finish building your system long before the minimum distance runs out—then if you hit the flow control button, you get all those wonderful extra points.

As you saw earlier, you can go to the Skill menu and choose any level you want. Pipe Dream then asks you for the password that you got from the bonus window in the level before. If you don't want to bother earning the real password, just hold down Ctrl-Alt-Shift *and* click on the OK button at the same time. Presto! All the way up to level 33 if you like! The new game starts right away, so don't congratulate yourself too long on beating the system. You can choose levels from the Skill menu lower than this level without having to supply a password, but you have to supply a password (or sneak around it) if you subsequently try to choose a higher level.

One way to spice up the game and keep yourself confused is to change the spare pipe bin. Usually the pipes move down the stack and you take them off the bottom. But if you're like a friend of Wes's, you'll want the pieces to come off the top of the bin. If you want to switch your bin around, you can go into the ENTPACK.INI file with the Windows Notepad and add the line "CheezHead = 1" under the [Pipe Dream] heading. When you're bored with taking the pieces off the top, change the entry to "Cheez-Head = 0" or remove it completely.

While you're in the ENTPACK.INI file, look for a line that says "WinPipe = 0." If you change the 0 to 1, the Pipe Dream icon in the upper corner of the window changes from a pipe with goo flowing out to a cross-section of someone's head. This icon, known affectionately as "Mr. Esophagus Man," was removed on the grounds of good taste: he vomits goo. No, that just wouldn't fly in the finished product, Microsoft felt, and it was replaced with the much more tasteful and well-mannered icon you're used to seeing. Unfortunately, this icon didn't show when the goo was about to flow out of the Start piece (you could tell how many seconds were left by how high Mr. Esophagus Man's, er, gorge had risen). After several requests, the icon was quietly added as a hidden feature, but not documented … until now.

RattlerRace

 attlerRace has been around in one form or another since before there were personal computers. Chris Fraley's goal was to write the game with his own twists. The basic scenario here is that you've got this rattlesnake ranch. Unfortunately, the little guys' feeding rooms are mined with a variety of hazards that can kill them while they're trying to eat their favorite food—apples. To top things off, the snakes don't see very well and they move quickly. Nice.

Object of the Game

The object of RattlerRace is to guide your snake so it can find and eat all the apples in the room and then get out an opening at the top without running into a wall (and dying) or being creamed by a bouncing ball (and dying) or colliding with another snake (and dying) or running into itself (you guessed it). You keep playing until you run out of snakes.

RattlerRace is one of the many games in the Entertainment Packs that you can't really "win." Sooner or later, you run out of snakes and the game is over. When that happens, the closing window melts and a Game Over message appears. If you have a high score, you can enter your name on the High Score table.

Opening window for Rattler Race

Game Window

When you load RattlerRace, you see only the RattlerRace logo screen. To start the game, choose New Game from the Game menu. The starting screen appears.

Below the menu bar on the left side is the spare-rattler pen. You start with three snakes. The numbers on the right side change as you play the game; they show you your score in seconds.

Just below the pen and the score (and right above the playing area) is a long bar that adds some extra excitement to the game. The amount of time it takes for the indicator to move from the right side of the bar to the left side is all the time your snake has to move to the next apple and eat it. If the time runs out, another three apples appear in the room.

The dark part of the window with the border is the room where the rattler is turned loose. There are walls built in the room, which you have to guide your snake around. At the bottom of the window, in the middle, you can see the snake coming out of its hole.

Play!

Starting the game. Double-click on the RattlerRace icon in the Entertainment Pack Two group window. When the RattlerRace logo screen appears, choose Balls from the Options menu and change the 1 to none by clicking the zero on the list. Choose Computer Snakes from the Options menu and do the same thing. Finally, choose Beginner from the top of the Options menu to set the game to its slowest speed.

Now that your options are set, you're ready to begin. Choose New from the Game menu, or press F2. The game displays the message "Level 01" in the playing area. (Levels are also called "rooms" in RattlerRace. They're the same thing.) Click on the message to start the snake out of the hole.

Start of a Rattler Race game

Moves. The rattler's always in motion, but his movements are random. You have to guide him toward the apples and away from hazards. You can use either the mouse or the keyboard to maneuver your rattler. The arrow keys herd him left, right, up, or down; the left and right mouse buttons to move him left and right. Controlling the snake takes some practice. If you turn it too sharply in a circle, it runs into itself and dies.

As soon as the rattler appears from the hole at the bottom of the screen, you're fighting the clock. If you run out of time, three more apples appear in the room. As the snake eats the apples, it grows longer, making it harder to maneuver. If you succeed in clearing all the apples, a snake hole appears at the top of the room. You have to guide the (now huge) snake into its new hole so you can move on to the next level in the game.

Hazards. Four hazards threaten your snake's life as it forages for apples: walls, computer snakes, bouncing balls, and your rattlesnake itself. If your snake encounters any of these hazards, it dies, and another snake crawls into the feeding room. The severity of these hazards depends on the skill level at which you're playing.

Skill levels. You can change four factors to increase the challenge as you get better at playing the game: speed, rooms, computer snakes, and bouncing balls.

Keyboard or mouse?

Rattler is one of the games in the Entertainment Packs that is much better when you play it with the keyboard. Using the arrow keys on either the numeric keypad or the T-shaped keypad, you can turn the snake in all four directions. If you use the mouse, you can only make the snake turn right with the right button or left with the left button. You can also press F1 for Help, F2 to start a new game, F3 to suspend a game, and Esc to shrink the game window to an icon. To quit the game, press Alt-F4.

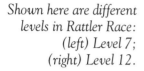

Shown here are different levels in Rattler Race: (left) Level 7; (right) Level 12.

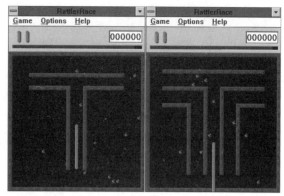

Speed. The first factor you should set is skill level, which really affects only speed. You can choose from four skill levels: Beginner (where the rattler moves slowly), Intermediate (medium speed), Advanced (too fast), or Expert (where you'd think your rattler was part Blue Racer). Choose the skill level you want from the Game menu.

Rooms. The game is set up to advance you from one room to the next, as you successfully guide your snakes around the hazards of the play area and let them escape out the top. After you're comfortable with the game, you can set it up to start at your favorite room. Just choose Room from the Options menu, then choose your favorite room from the list that appears. (Chris Fraley put this feature in because he wanted to be able to skip to a favorite room without having to play through the lower rooms.) When you start the game again, you're in the room you chose.

The game gives you thirty rooms/levels to choose from, set up in groups of five. You can see this best by choosing Starting Room from the Options menu and clicking on the middle of the Room scroll bar. As you do this, the rooms go up by five. Rooms 1, 6, 11, 16, and 21 have pairs of vertical bars on either side of the screen. Rooms 2, 7, 12, 17, and 22 are T-shaped. Rooms 3, 8, 13, 18, and 23 look like an arch. Rooms 4, 9, 14, 19, and 24 are brackets in a nested box. Rooms 5, 10, 15, 20, and 25 are made of nested L-shapes. Because the shapes in a series are similar, once you develop a strategy for solving the first room in a series, you should be able to use the same strategy for the rest of the rooms in the series.

Rooms 26 through 30 don't follow the pattern of the previous rooms. Room 26 is like two snakes intertwined. Rooms 27 and 29 are very similar. Room 28 is very hard because of the zig-zags, but it has lots of single-dot walls that change into clock faces. To win in room 28, you need to develop techniques that apply specifically to this room: how to get from one square to another quickly.

Room 30 looks like it's totally random, but it isn't, quite: if you look carefully, you'll see that the pattern has no dead ends. Chris's original version of RattlerRace had a harder version of room 30. The blocks were fairly small, and tough to avoid. Chris says that he actually won it, once, at the slow speed. Room 30's been changed since then to what you see now, but Chris warns, "Anyone who wants to try room 30 should remove the bouncing balls and the computer snakes, and try it on the slow speed. That's the only realistic way to finish this room."

Computer snakes. Computer snakes are there to make your life miserable: their raison d'être is to get in your way. Through the Options menu, set the number of computer snakes you want, from zero to three snakes.

A computer snake does one of three things: it wanders about randomly, it wanders about randomly until it spots

Clock faces

Some rooms, such as 15 and 28, have a lot of single-dot walls. Every so often, a single-block wall turns into a clock face. If your snake eats the clock face as if it were an apple, the timer at the top of the screen stops. This gives you extra time to move your snake around. Be careful, though: a clock face can change back at the last minute, and your rattler runs right into a wall! (If you watch the demo screen long enough, you'll see a clock face appear. That's what you're looking for.)

an apple nearby (in which case it eats it), or it makes a beeline for your rattler's head. Computer snakes are fickle things: every five seconds or so, the computer snake reconsiders what it's doing, and (possibly) does something else. At the lower levels, the snake is most likely to move randomly, and maybe eat apples. At the higher levels, the snake likes to chase you. The important thing is to recognize what the snake is doing so you aren't surprised by it.

Bouncing balls. Like computer snakes, the bouncing balls are there to make trouble. They appear out of nowhere and carom randomly about the snakes' feeding room. If one of them bounces onto a snake, the snake dies. Set the number of balls you want, from zero to three, on the Options menu.

Endgame. RattlerRace is over when all your rattlers buy the farm. The window image melts (it takes an annoyingly long time), then the "Game over" message appears. If you want to short-circuit the endless melt process, you have to press the Esc key. To shrink the window to an icon while it's doing this, you have to press Esc twice: once to interrupt the screen melting and the second time to shrink the window.

Things can be even worse, if (gasp!) you achieved a high score: you may have to press Esc as many as four times to shrink the window. To quit RattlerRace, double-click on the top-left button of the game window.

Scoring and Winning

You get one point for each apple your rattler eats, and five for moving to the next room. If your rattler dies and you get another from the pen, you get the score for the apples the new rattler eats. You also get the points if time runs out and your snake eats the three extra apples.

Tips, Traps, and Sneaky Tricks

Just about the only help this game gives you is the Pause key, F3. (You can also choose Pause from the Game menu).

In the beginning you may need time to think about your next move. Just press F3, decide what you want to do, and press F3 again to resume the action.

As you accumulate points, you can actually earn more rattlers. You get the first extra snake at 50 points, then at every 100 points thereafter. Additional snakes appear at the top of the screen above the timer.

You'll remember that the rattler grows as it feeds. As it gets longer and longer, it can get more difficult to maneuver out of tight places. One tip is maneuver the snake so that it eats an apple on its way to the next apple, so you don't have that extra length in the way. This becomes more important as the length of your snake increases and the size of the rooms decreases. For the same reason, you should eat the apples in the small rooms first.

You can use either relative movement or absolute movement with the keyboard. Choose Relative Movement from the Options menu to switch between the two. Relative movement means that the snake moves to right or left relative to its current motion when you press the right or left arrows. (The up and down arrows have no effect in relative movement.) Absolute movement means that the snake moves in the direction of the arrow you press regardless of the current direction of the snake.

If you want to become a really good player, use the keyboard instead of the mouse. Also, don't use relative movement; it's very hard to press the same key twice in a row, whereas with absolute movement, you're always hitting two different keys to reverse the snake's direction (crucial at the higher levels).

If you're using a VGA monitor in 1024x768 mode, you have a couple of extra choices on the Options menu: Small and Large. These let you choose small or large window sizes for the playing area. The large size is easier to see.

CHAPTER 16

Rodent's Revenge

You're a rat in world full of cats and traps. You have to watch out for killer yarn balls and sink holes. There's nowhere to hide, and you can't run away. What are you going to do? You're going to turn the tables and trap the cats. You're better than Ben, smarter than Willard, and more devious than Templeton. You are RODENT!

Rodent's Revenge is a real video game in the best tradition, the brainchild of Chris Fraley (who also wrote RattlerRace). You have to trap the cats before the cats eat you, while avoiding holes, yarnballs, and rat traps. And you have to do it quickly.

Object of the Game

The object of Rodent's Revenge is to trap the cats as quickly as possible without getting eaten. You keep playing until you run out of rats.

Game Window

The game opens onto a matrix of light-green boxes, fifteen to a side. These are your only defense and your only weapon against the cats. You trap cats by pushing the boxes around.

Rodent's Revenge before the game begins

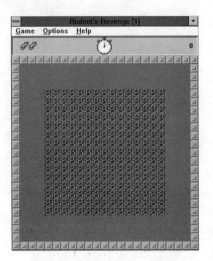

On the gray bar above the playing field, you can see how many chances you have by the number of rats lined up. In the center of the bar is a stopwatch to remind you that you have to move fast. It ticks away while you play. On the right is your score. In the title bar, the number in parentheses after "Rodent's Revenge" is the skill level number.

Although you can't maximize Rodent's Revenge to fill the entire screen, you can choose Large Size on the Options menu to fill about a third of the screen. Small Size can be hard to see because it is so tiny, but it does hide easily underneath an open group window. (Like RattlerRace, Small Size and Large Size won't show up with some lower-resolution monitors).

Play!

Starting the game. Double-click the Rodent's Revenge icon in the Entertainment Pack Two group window to start the game. Although the game opens to a play area, you need to choose New Game or press F2 to get a game started.

The game opens with one rat in the middle of the play area. A very excited puss waits at the edge of the light-green boxes for a chance to breach the defense and pounce on that succulent rat. As time goes on, more cats hear about the prize and show up to try their luck. The rat can shove those columns of boxes around, but the cats can't. This is the rodent's only advantage in the game.

Trapping a cat

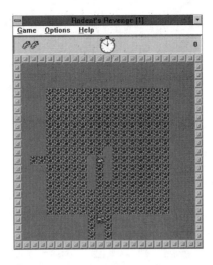

Moves. You're a rat, and rats can go anywhere: left, right, up, down, or diagonally. Use the numeric key pad to move in the direction indicated by the arrows. Use the four corner keys (1, 3, 7, and 9) to move diagonally.

If there are light-green boxes in the direction you're going, they move when you push them. Although you can push them, you can't scamper over the top of them. This can cause problems if you move a box or boxes up against a wall. You may have to take a detour to get where you're going.

Be careful. If you try to trap a cat and it has somewhere else to jump, it will. Cats can move diagonally; they'll jump over and eat you quicker than you can say "Monterey Jack."

Trap the cats by maneuvering the light-green boxes until the cat is stuck in a one-by-one space. This isn't too hard, because the cats aren't very bright. Until there's a

Going for the cheese

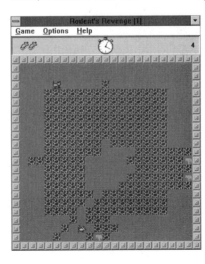

clear path, they tend to just move back and forth within a few squares in the same row or column the rat's in. Once they've got a path, though, they're fast. If a cat catches you, you die.

When a cat is trapped, it does what every cat does when it has nothing better to do with its time: it curls up and falls asleep. When you trap all the cats, they turn into pieces of cheese. More cats show up, but follow your rat nature and go back after the cheese. It's worth extra points. Be careful, because you can squish the cheese before you get a chance to eat it if you push a box into its space. You have to push a row or two of light-green boxes out of your way to nab your dinner.

Skill levels. You go to the next skill level when you've trapped all the cats on the current level. You keep this up until you run out of rats. Levels are set up in groups of six. Level 1 has nothing but green blocks. Level 2 has mostly green blocks with a few immovable gray blocks in the way. Level 3 is a random assortment of green blocks with some gray blocks. Level 4 is a checkerboard of green blocks. Level 5 is a random assortment of mostly gray blocks, some green blocks, and mouse holes. Level 6 is a checkerboard of gray blocks with some green blocks.

The blocks in level 7 are arranged in a square like those in level 1. Each level thereafter looks like the one six levels before it, but there are more hazards, and the cats move a little faster each time. Because the shapes in a series are similar, once you develop a strategy for solving the first level in a series, you should be able to use the same strategy for the rest of the levels in the series. The goal is still the same though: trap the cats and get the cheese.

Rodent's Revenge normally starts at level 1, but you can set it to start at any level. To pick a level, choose Level on the Options Menu and type the level you want in the

The levels have different layouts.

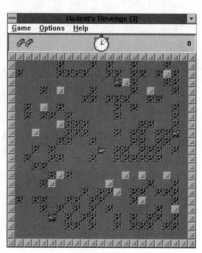

box. From now on, Rodent's Revenge will start using the level you just entered.

Speed. Pick the speed at which you and the cat move by choosing the appropriate one on the Options menu. The slowest speed is Snail. This is a good speed to learn how things work. It's even a bit of a challenge until you're more accustomed to everything. The speeds—Slow, Medium, High, and Blazing—build from there, with each one a little faster than the one before. "Blazing" is aptly named because things really do heat up at that speed.

Hazards. Life is not all trapping cats and eating cheese. As you go up levels, you run into hazards that make your quest to trap the cats more difficult. If it's any consolation, you don't see any new hazards at the levels past 7—but the old hazards get more plentiful.

Gray blocks. The immovable gray blocks that first appear on level 2 make it harder to move the green blocks any way you want. It takes longer to maneuver around them to set up a good trap.

What are the yarnballs going to do next?

The yarnballs work with different algorithms for each level (very much like the computer snakes in RattlerRace). The three basic things they'll do is: shoot off in random directions at random intervals, shoot off in random directions at random intervals unless the rat crosses their line of fire (in which case they go for the rat), or aim for the rat whenever they can. As you go up levels, the yarnballs are more likely to start hunting rats than being random. And, just to make your life difficult, some of the yarnballs on the higher levels fire when the rat is *one square away* from the yarnball's line of fire. Why? Because this makes it harder to jump out of the way when you see a yarnball coming at you — you're just as likely to jump into the path as out of it.

Sink holes. Starting at level 4, you've got sink holes to contend with. If you fall into a hole, you're stuck there for up to ten seconds, during which time you are a sitting duck (or possibly, a sitting rat). If green boxes fall into a hole, they're lost forever.

Yarnballs. Yarnballs are mobile hazards that first appear on level 5. If a rat gets hit by a yarnball, it dies. Finally, rat traps start appearing on level 7. Rat traps are immovable (just like gray blocks).

Endgame. When the game is over, you get a "Game Over" message and everything on the playing field melts down and leaks off the bottom of your screen. This is cool to watch once or twice, but you can skip it by pressing Esc as soon as the screen starts melting.

Scoring and Winning

You can't really win Rodent's Revenge. Sooner or later, the cats, the traps, and the yarnballs will get you, and your last rat is sent to the Big Cheese Warehouse in the Sky. Aim for the highest score you can.

Every time you eat a cheese you get 100 points plus a bonus for the level you're on. When you finish a level, you get 100 points times the level number and a 100-point bonus. So if you finish level 12, you score 1300 points. Speed adds to your score—the quicker you finish a level, the more points you get. You get more points for playing at the higher speeds as well, but you have to earn it: the cats move awfully fast at Blazing!

When you earn a high score, a dialog box appears titled "Rodent's High Score" with the message, "You have achieved a high score! Please enter your name:" If you were the last person to get high score, your name is already in the box. Just click OK or press Enter. If someone else's name is there, delete that name and replace it with yours. The Rodent High Score's Hall of Fame Box appears and you can see your position among the high scores overall and for the day. To clear the high scores, click the Clear Scores button. To display the current high scores at any time, choose High Scores from the Game menu.

Tips, Traps, and Sneaky Tricks

The gray blocks that get in your way can actually be an advantage. You may be able to trap a cat against a gray block without having to moving green blocks all the way to the wall. You can also use the rat traps this way.

Sink holes vanish after the rat gets free. If you have sink holes in the middle of the grid of green boxes when you start a level, you may want to intentionally fall into them just to get rid of them. Rat traps also vanish after they've caught you, but the cost to get rid of one of them is high.

As you move the green boxes around, try not to clear a path for the cats. Once you're on the run it's really hard to find time to trap a cat. Also, new cats sneak in from the sides when you're not looking and come up behind you. You've got to watch the entire board at once. There are more cats than you might think!

[XREF4B]If you're feeling really macho (or masochistic), you can use an undocumented feature to go past level

From the keyboard

There's an ironic twist here—you can't use the mouse to play *Rodent's* Revenge. You use the numeric keypad or the arrow keys to move your rats in any direction you like. (The Num Lock key must be off!) You do best with the ones on the numeric keypad because they let you move diagonally as well as up and down. Rodent's Revenge also provides the other standard keyboard shortcuts:

F2	starts a new game.
F3	pauses the game and resumes the game when it is paused.
Esc	instantly minimizes the game.
Alt-F4	exits Rodent's Revenge.
Ctrl-Shift-Pgup	goes down levels (towards level 1).
Ctrl-Shift-Pgdn	goes up levels (towards level 50).

50. Choose Level on the Options Menu and set the level to 50, then press Ctrl-Shift-Pgdn to go up as many levels as you like. Chris Fraley's only comment on the levels past 50 is "Play at the high levels is kind of difficult." Stick with Snail speed unless you're just interested in seeing how fast the rat can be dismembered by the cats and the yarnballs.

CHAPTER 17

Stones

tones is similar to Taipei from Microsoft Entertainment Pack, Volume One, but now instead of trying to take the tiles off the board, you're trying to put them on. You're going to get to play matchmaker (in fact, Stones is based on a Chinese game called "Love"). As any good matchmaker knows, an exact match isn't necessary; just a few qualities in common will do the trick. And then of course there are always those people who just get along with everyone.

Stones was written by Michael C. Miller. He got the idea when he saw his roommate's parents (who are Chinese) playing the game with a mah jongg set. He picked up most of the rules from them. The game changed some as he was writing it. Stones is Michael's second Windows program. The first was a simple "shuffle-the-number" puzzle. Michael says to keep an eye out for more games he's written.

Object of the Game

To win this game, you have to place ninety "stones" of various colors and patterns on the playing grid in the fastest time possible. Sounds easy, but the game has strict rules about how you arrange the stones.

Game Window

The Stones window opens with six stones already placed on a ten-by-ten grid.

Start of Stones game

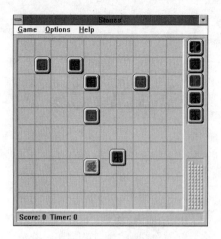

Your score and your time appear in the lower-left corner of the Stones window. The next five stones you need to place are lined up on the right side of the window. The bottom stone is the next one that you'll put on the board after you drop the cursor stone.

You don't need to count the stones to know how close you are to winning. All you need to do is look at the gray progress block in the lower-right corner, under the line of stones waiting to be placed. The game starts with some of the stones missing from the block—they're already on the playing surface. Each time you place a stone, another stone disappears from the block. When you get close to the end of the game, you'll be able to tell how many still need to go on the board. If you should lose, you can also tell how close you came to winning.

Play!

Starting the Game. Start Stones by double-clicking the Stones icon in the Entertainment Pack Two group window. Stones opens directly into a game. When the cursor is on the grid, it becomes the first stone to put on the board. When you move the cursor off the board, it goes back to its regular shape.

Next to the playing surface are the next five stones you'll place. The bottom stone is the one you'll have to place after

Stones game in progress

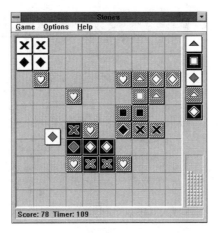

you place the cursor stone. When you place a stone, the next one automatically becomes the cursor. Each of the stones moves down in the row and a new stone pops to the top of the line.

The timer doesn't start until you place the first stone.

Moves. To place a stone, move it where you want it and click to drop it. You can't place a stone off by itself; it has to be next to at least one other stone. You can place a stone next to any other stone that matches it with two or more attributes. When you place a stone next to more than one other stone, it has to match all the stones touching its sides.

Wild stones are not loners. They can get along with anyone, but they have to be placed next to at least one stone. Try not to waste them. They're very important when you need to bridge a gap in matching attributes.

Stone Sets. Stones comes with five stone sets. To pick a new stone set, choose Stone Styles from the Options menu. A box comes up with the wild stone (like a wild card) from each set displayed across the top. To see what the set looks like, click the wild stone. The full set appears in rows below the wild stones. When you decide which one you like, click OK and that set of stones appears on the board. You can do this any time, even in the middle of a game.

Stone sets to choose from

The stone set with the heart is designed for people using mono screens, such as on a laptop. The other styles won't show up well on a monochrome display.

Each stone set has twelve wild stones, which can be placed next to any stone. When you choose Stone Set from the Options menu, each of the sets is represented by its wild stone design.

Stone Attributes. Each stone set has three attributes. In some of the stone sets, these are two colors (for example, foreground and background colors, or top stripe and bottom stripe colors) and then several different designs. So a stone in one of these sets could match another based on foreground color and exact design, or they could have different designs but match on foreground and background

Making more stone sets

You can actually create more stone sets and load them as STONE.DLLs. The DLLs are just a bunch of bitmaps that display the stones. If you're used to programming dynamic linked libraries for Windows, you can match the image formatting and create your own.

colors. In other sets, you have to match directions and designs. When you look at each stone set, the three attributes are obvious.

You have to have a color monitor to see the attributes of all but one stone set. Even with a color monitor, you may need to adjust the brightness or contrast to see them clearly.

Options. If you don't like being under the gun, turn the timer off by choosing Timer from the Options Menu. You can also turn off the illegal-move beep by choosing Beep from the Options menu. Turn off the background grid by choosing Show Grid from the Options menu. All the selections on the Options menu can be used any time during the game.

Endgame. Continue to place stones until you win or get a box that says, "The next stone will not fit on the board." The game's over. To play another round, choose New Game from the Game menu or press F2.

Scoring and Winning

You score two points when you place a stone on the board. If the stone is a wild stone, these are the only two points

---

From the keyboard

To play Stones from the keyboard, use the arrow keys to move the stone you're about to place. To drop the stone, press Enter. Press F2 for a new game, F3 to pause, F1 for help, and Backspace to undo your last move. Pressing Esc minimizes the screen quickly (should you need to do that for no particular reason). Pressing Esc also stops the timer until you maximize the screen again.

You can choose a new stone set with the keyboard, too. In the Stone Select dialog box (Alt-O, S), use the arrow keys to highlight the stone set you want and then press the spacebar to show all the stones in the set. Press Enter when you're happy with the stone set you chose.

you'll score. Other stones get two more points for each adjacent stone that has at least one different attribute.

If you place any stone except a wild stone next to two other stones you get three bonus points. If you place it next to three stones, you get five bonus points, and if it fills the hole inside four stones, you get ten bonus points.

You can lose points, too. Every time you try to put a stone where it doesn't fit, you lose one point. Each time you use Undo or Revert Position, you lose two points. The score even goes into negative numbers, so think about your move before you drop a stone.

Michael Miller says he wins about half the time. He also says that not all the games are winnable, because the pieces are placed randomly. He originally tried to program Stones so that it guaranteed that every game was winnable, but the program took way too long to run, so he figured that he'd leave it alone. Michael says "There's always a good chance the game is winnable."

When you win, a message box says, "Congratulations, all stones have been placed!" Click OK, but watch out— the result of any good bit of matchmaking is offspring. Suddenly, your stones are multiplying all over the board and soon the entire window is full of stones.

Trips, Traps, and Sneaky Tricks

While you're new to the game, just put stones anywhere they fit. You don't win many games this way, but you get pretty high scores because the stones touch other stones with different attributes and you learn how to match them.

After you've played more, find an attribute that's easy to recognize and group around it. Watch the edges as you do this. You don't want to end up with empty spaces that can hold only wild stones. Michael recommends this strategy for finishing the game.

Place stones carefully around the edges of a group. For example, if you've been matching on background color and design, you'll want to put stones that also match on foreground color around the edge of the group. This lets you match edge stones based on any of the three attributes.

Try to find somewhere else to place a stone before using up the valuable spaces next to a wild stone. Remember, eventually you're going to end up with a stone that just won't fit anywhere else, and if you don't have space next to a wild stone, you lose the game.

For a challenge, pretend the axes of the board are boundaries. Line up stones on either axis (vertical or horizontal), based on one group of attributes, such as background color. Base the other axis on a different group of attributes. Now place the stones in rows from there. This is hard, but your score goes pretty high.

If you get interrupted during a game, choose Pause from the Game menu or press F3. This stops the timer and places a "cover" over the board—a slick way to show that the game is paused. (It also prevents you from studying the board with the timer off, for those cads who might stoop to cheating in such a low fashion.) To restart the game, choose Pause from the Game menu again.

If you place a stone and then decide you'd like it somewhere else, undo your last move by choosing Undo Last Place from the Game menu.

The Save Position and Revert Position options on the Game menu can come in handy. Once you're close to winning, use Save Position to save the board. By using Revert Position, you can keep trying different stone placements until you find one that works. But there is a trap! The game remembers your last saved position, even if you quit the game. If you think you've saved and you haven't, you may experience a time warp and suddenly find yourself thrown into a completely different game from your past.

The Save Position option also lets you see both of the victory scenarios easily. Save the game right before you place the last stone. You then see the "Congratulations" dialog box. When you click on OK, you see one or the other of the two endings to the game. You can then use the Revert

Position option to put you back to right before you won the game, and do it again. You can replay winning the game until you've seen both endings and you've glutted yourself on your victory.

How to cheat at Stones   You can't. Even pausing the game puts a cover over the board so you can't see it. Ain't it disgusting?

CHAPTER 18

Tut's Tomb

ut's Tomb is an electronic version of the traditional Pyramid card game, also known as Thirteens. The old card-table version of Pyramid gave the player fifty-to-one odds of winning. Tut's Tomb is about as tough to beat, not because it requires you to be smarter than you are, but because winning this game depends largely on the luck of the deal.

Rick LaPlante and others developed Tut's Tomb as a software engineering class project. While other students were writing boring stuff like grading systems and videotape rental programs, Rick dreamed of doing a Windows game. He wrote the first version with classmates Warren Nolder and Don Schiele. The development effort followed the typical pattern: task one was to design team T-shirts. When the real work of writing code was finally done (with Rick's wife Judith providing user feedback and technical consulting), the game was a success. The teacher passed them—with a plea for a "Teacher Wins" option in the next version.

Object of the Game

The object of Tut's Tomb is to clear all the cards from the tableau to a discard pile at the top of the game window. To do this, you have to match pairs of free cards that equal thirteen when you add their ranks together. Sounds easy, but it's not, because you can't play a card that's partly covered by another card.

Opening layout
for Tut's Tomb

Game Window

The game deals a pyramid of twenty-eight cards, starting with one card at the top. The pyramid has seven rows, and the bottom row has seven cards. The remaining twenty-four cards appear face down in the stock in the top-left corner of the game window. In the top-right corner of the window is an empty discard pile, where you put the cards as you move them from the tableau.

Below the title bar of the game window are the Game and Help menus. The Game menu lets you start a new game, choose options, exit, and execute other commands. Get to the Help screens by clicking the Help menu label or pressing F1.

The message bar at the bottom of the game window shows your score. At the beginning of the game its says "-28," which is your starting score. It means there are twenty-eight cards remaining in the tableau. You work your way up from the basement in this one.

Play!

Starting the game. Click on the Tut's Tomb icon (shaped like a pyramid) in the Entertainment Pack Two group window. The game opens and deals your first hand.

Moves. Tut's Tomb gives you three basic moves.

Flip your kings. First, find any kings and click on them to send them to the discard pile. You don't need to click on a second card to get rid of a king to the discard pile, because it's worth thirteen points by itself. Kings are "free" cards.

Make a pilgrimage to the pyramid. Second, look in the pyramid for pairs of exposed cards that total thirteen. To flip a pair to the discard pile, click on one of the cards; it changes to inverse video. Then click on the other card in the pair. If you click on two cards that don't add up to thirteen, the highlighted card returns to normal. You can choose pairs of any suit and any color, in any order you want. The cards you pair up must be fully exposed on the pyramid—they can't be covered (even partly) by any other card. For instance, when the game starts you can use any cards in the bottom row, but none of the cards underneath.

Take stock. When you run out of legal free pairs in the tableau, your third kind of move is to pair a free card from the tableau with one from the stock. Again, the pair has to equal thirteen when you add the ranks of the two cards together. Click on the stock in the top-left corner of the window to turn over the first three cards. You can play only the top card of the draw at any time, but once you've played it, you can play the next card down. Click on the stock for more cards. When you run out of cards in the stock, you see a green "O" (just like in Solitaire). You can click on the "O" to turn the stock over and go through it again.

Think carefully about your matches if you have a choice of cards to play. Try to pick a card that exposes another playable card in the tableau or a card that's different from

What is 13, besides unlucky?

Aces are worth 1, deuces are 2, and so on. Jacks count as 11, queens as 12. Typical pairs of 13 are a 9 and a 4, a jack and a deuce, or a queen and an ace. Kings are worth 13 by themselves.

Tut's Tomb game
in progress

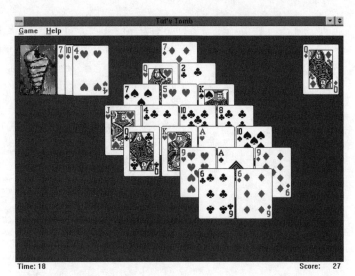

the other free cards. This gives you the most options for pairing cards and increases your chances of winning.

Also, be warned: you can right-click anywhere in the window to flip the next three cards from the stock. However, it's really easy to hit the right mouse button—and there's no way to go backwards. So if you have a twitchy finger, you may want to flip the cards by clicking on the stock back, even though it means you have to move the pointer more.

Keep turning over the stock and making pairs of cards until all the cards in the pyramid are gone or you can't play anymore.

Options. Customize your game from the Game Options menu. You can specify either one or three cards turned over at a time from the stock by choosing Draw One or Draw Three. The Timed Game option shows the elapsed time at the bottom of the screen (the timer keeps track of when you last won the game or when you last started, whichever is the most recent). Beep just beeps when you try to make an illegal pair.

You can change the card backs to any of the Windows card backs (described in the chapter on Solitaire near the beginning of the book) by clicking the Deck option under the Game menu.

Standard scoring lets you turn the stock over as many times as you want and scores using standard rules. Casino scoring uses Casino rules (see the Scoring and Winning section, below, for more information). Note that if you change the Timed Game, Draw, or Scoring options during a game, Tut's Tomb deals a new hand.

Endgame. Most people play Tut's Tomb to get all the cards off the pyramid. When you do this, you get a dialog box that tells you your score. When you click OK, a pyramid appears on the screen. The front slowly opens, and the King of Clubs slowly comes up and starts bouncing around the window. You'll also find that if you minimize the game or shift to something else while the King is bouncing around the screen, the pyramid doesn't reappear. You only see the King from its current position. It keeps bouncing until you start a new game or exit the program.

When you lose, nothing obvious happens; you just can't make any more moves. To start another game, press F2 or choose Deal from the Game menu. If you want to start with a clean slate, choose New session. The game clears your old scores and deals another round.

Scoring and Winning

Like Solitaire, Tut's Tomb has three different scoring options that let you tailor the scoring to your anxiety level about being in debt. Choose Options from the Game menu. You can choose Standard scoring (the default), Casino scoring (a little like Vegas scoring in Solitaire), or None.

From the keyboard

To get help, press F1. To start a new game, press F2. Press F3 to pause the game. Press ESC to minimize the screen if the boss appears suddenly. This won't work immediately if the King of Clubs is just coming out of the pyramid.

The option None has no scoring. You can just play, without winning or losing any money. The Standard scoring option lets you win a little and lose a little, but you won't have to hock your Tut memorabilia to get back home. Casino scoring is for the stout of heart—you can win big or lose it all.

Standard scoring runs on a point system. You are charged 28 points to deal a new game, one point for each card turned over in the draw, and ten points when you recycle the deck. Also, if you chose the Timed game option you're charged one point for every ten seconds that the game is in play—so speed counts in the Timed game. You earn thirteen points each time you make a match. The nice part of the Standard scoring is that your score isn't carried over from one game to the next. So if you win a game (and get to see what's inside the tomb) you have really won the game.

To play Tut's Tomb with Casino rules, choose Casino scoring from the Game Options menu. Although the Casino layout looks the same as the standard game, the Casino game limits the number of times you can run through the stock. When you go through the stock the last time, you see a red "X" instead of a green "O" on the empty stock pile. The "X" means that you can't go through the stock again: once you finish moving the cards on the tableau, the game's over. You can go through the stock either one or three times, depending on whether you pick Draw One or Draw Three on the Game Options menu.

Casino scoring is based on dollars rather than points. Furthermore, the dollars you win or lose are carried from one game to the next (or until you click the New session

About the endgame

Why does the King of Clubs come out of the tomb? Rick says it's because the club on the card looks like a four-leaf clover (for luck), and the King, because it *is* the tomb of a king, after all. Now you know.

option under the Game menu). The dollars charged and
won are somewhat similar to the Standard scoring. You're
charged $28 to deal a new game, $1 for each card drawn,
$10 to recycle the deck, and $5 for each card that's left in
the pyramid at the end of the game. If you chose a timed
game, you are charged $1 for each ten seconds of the game.
In Casino scoring, you earn $13 each time you send a pair
of cards to the discard pile.

Tips, Traps, and Sneaky Tricks

Try to make your matches from the cards in the pyramid
first, rather than matching from the stock. The exception
is when you're playing a timed game with the Standard
scoring. Then it may be to your advantage to make lots of
pairs fast any way you can and redeal, because you aren't
penalized for the cards left in the pyramid.

Don't be too quick to use up the kings in the stock. They
aren't hurting anything just sitting there, and you can
change the cards that appear as the top card by removing
a single king from near the start of the stock. This can be
very helpful near the end of the game when you need one
particular card.

Some games are clearly unwinnable. For example, if you
have all four tens in the first two rows and some or all of

More history

Tut's Tomb has had more names than any other game in
the Microsoft Entertainment Packs. The game was
originally called "Coffee Break," because it was a game for
you to play on your coffee break. This was rejected as not
being descriptive enough. Rick then suggested "Pyramid,"
but Microsoft's legal department didn't like that. Legal
then suggested "Thirteens," but Rick felt that that would
be too boring. Legal finally provided a list of names,
including "King Tut," "Ramses," "Pharoah's Revenge,"
"Tut," and "Tut's Tomb," and told Rick to pick one. Rick
settled on "Tut's Tomb."

the threes are pinned under them, you can't possibly win because the cards are blocking their mates. With Standard or no scoring, you may not even want to waste your time with this game. Just press F2 again and get on with your life. On the other hand, in Casino rules, it costs $5 for every card left when you redeal, but you make $13 for every match you make. So, if you're playing for a high score, make every match possible even if a game is clearly unwinnable.

With the Draw One option, you should use cards from the stock as soon as possible. Don't wait; you only get to go through the deck once.

Part 4

The Microsoft Entertainment Pack: Volume Three

Microsoft had too many games to include in Volume Two, so they created the Microsoft Entertainment Pack: Volume Three at the same time. Volume Three includes:

more...	⬇

CHAPTER 19

Fuji Golf

 s you scramble to make your tee time, do you ever wonder how it would feel to have your own year-round golf course? For the price of your Microsoft Entertainment Pack, you have acquired a chunk of prime real estate—your own golf course.

Object of the Game

Fuji Golf is a lot like regular golf: you hit the ball and then you walk after it. The idea is to strike that tiny ball with a long, awkward metal pole so that the ball goes into an almost equally tiny hole very far away in as few strokes as possible. Eighteen times. Unlike most other games, the fewer points you score, the better you get to feel about yourself. As you get to know the course, you can lower your score and rise higher in the tournament rankings. One advantage of Fuji Golf is that you don't have to wear ugly plaid pants while playing it.

Game Window

The game window is dominated by two views of the first hole. The view on the left is a perspective, or three-dimensional, view. On the right is the aerial view. In between the two views is a thin vertical bar, the power indicator, which lets you determine how hard you hit the ball. Just below the bar is the Backswing button, with which you swat the ball.

Teeing off at the first hole

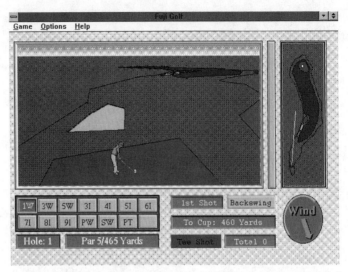

At lower-left is the selection of clubs: the 1, 3, and 5 woods, the 3 through 9 irons, the pitching wedge, the sand wedge, and the putter. The button for the club you're currently using looks as if it's been pressed in. Below and to the right of the buttons for the clubs is information on the current hole: the par, which shot you're on, the distance to the cup, the location of the current shot, and how many strokes above par your score is. At the lower-right corner is the wind indicator, showing the wind's current direction and approximate speed.

In the menu bar are the Game, Options, and Help menu labels, which let you start, pause, or quit a game, look at scores, or get Help.

Terrain and hazards of the course. Before you play, you need to understand the territory of the golf course. There are seven different types of terrain or hazard: the Tee, the Fairway, the Rough, the Green, Sand Trap, Water, and the ever-popular Out of Bounds.

The *tee* is the light-green rectangle where you hit your first shot for a hole.

The *fairway* is the medium-green area that takes up most of the course. If you can't make it to the green on your first shot, you want to land on the fairway because the low grass lets you hit the ball cleanly.

The *rough* is the strip of dark-green grass surrounding the fairway. If you land in the rough, you're going to have to hit the ball harder for the same distance, because the grass is longer on the rough than on the fairway.

The *green* is the light green area (the same color as the tee) that surrounds the hole, or *cup*. The green is always kept well-trimmed and smooth, so a little stroke goes a long way. Always use the putter on the green.

Sand traps (also known as *bunkers*) are the bright-white patches of sand in the fairway or near the green. If you land in the sand trap, you have to hit the ball very hard with the sand wedge to get out of the trap and back onto the fairway.

Water hazards are shown as blue. Water hazards can be on the fairway or out of bounds (but conveniently placed to catch balls that come in that direction). If your ball goes into the water, you are penalized one stroke and must play the ball from its point of entry to the water hazard.

Out of bounds is the brick-red area surrounding all the other terrain just described. If your ball goes out of bounds, the game penalizes you one stroke. You have to begin that stroke over again from the spot where you were before you went out of bounds.

Play!

Starting the game. Start Fuji Golf by double-clicking the Fuji Golf icon in the Entertainment Pack Three group window. The Fuji Golf course appears, a full eighteen-hole course and lavish clubhouse nestled on the foothills below majestic Mt. Fuji. Begin the round by clicking Start New Round under the picture. A dialog box appears asking for your name. Enter your name and click OK. (The very first time you play Fuji Golf after installing it, you see a dialog box with some tips on playing. Just click on "Continue" to get on with the game.) The first hole appears.

Moves. Take your first shot from the tee. Before you tee off, look at the wind indicator. The arrow points in the direction the wind is blowing, and its thickness is a relative measure of how strong the wind is. The wind direction and speed change with each hole. If the wind is blowing at an angle across the direction of the ball, you may want to adjust your aim.

The game proposes a shot direction, as seen in the aerial view as a white line from your current position. You can adjust this by moving the pointer (which turns into a golf ball) on the aerial view over the point you at which you want to aim. When you click, the white aiming line shifts accordingly. Next, choose your club.

Now that you have your shot all set up, you're ready to swing. Start your backswing by clicking on the Backswing button. (Actually, you can start your backswing by clicking anywhere on the window except on the perspective or aerial views.) The Backswing indicator is replaced by the message "Hit Ball," and a column of small red rectangles moves up the power indicator—pretty fast. The more red

Choosing a club

If you haven't played golf before, there are two things you should know about golf clubs. Woods hit longer than irons. The larger the number of the club (wood or iron), the higher the ball goes ... and the less distance down the fairway it travels. (Getting a lot of lift to the ball also lets it get blown around by the wind.)

Depending on the wind direction, you get between 200 and 250 yards when you tee off using the 1 wood. Be sure to factor the distance in to your calculations so that you don't go out-of-bounds. On par 3 holes, you may use a 3 wood or even a 5 wood so you don't overshoot the hole. But don't be afraid to experiment: the choice of club is often a matter of personal preference. Learn to choose clubs based on the way you like to play.

rectangles are in the power indicator, the harder you're going to hit the ball. When teeing off for the first hole (which is a par 5 about 465 yards away), you want to hit the ball as hard as you can. Click the mouse again when the rectangles completely fill the indicator (this takes a little practice to get your timing just perfect).

As soon as you click the Backswing button the second time, the golfer in the perspective view swings and clobbers the ball. You can watch the ball's progress down the fairway on the perspective view and the aerial view, where it appears as a red dot. The view changes and you're ready for your next shot.

Second shot on the fairway

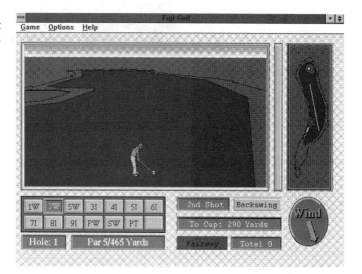

Now you see the hole from the perspective of your ball's new position, and you're using a different club. Which one you use depends on where you are with respect to the cup, and where the ball is lying. When you're just starting out, use the suggested club. Be aware, though, that although your caddy is pretty sharp, he doesn't get paid much and occasionally recommends a club that's not the best for the situation. You can choose another club yourself by clicking on the appropriate button (the pointer becomes a club).

As you continue to take your shots (closer and closer to the cup, you hope), you see the number of shots logged in the Shots tally in the center of the window just below the perspective view. When you get to the green, a second indicator appears in the lower right corner of the perspective view. This is the break indicator. It shows which way the ball is likely to "break"—that is, to curve. Like the wind indicator, the thickness of the arrow gives you an idea of how severe the break is likely to be.

On the green (note the break indicator)

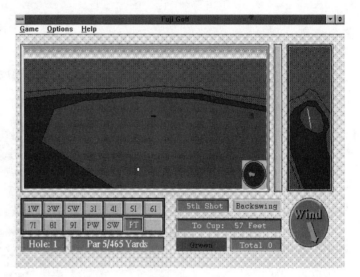

Use a putter when you get to the green. When you finally sink your ball in the cup, you see your score for the hole appear in a dialog box in the center of the Fuji Golf window, along with a comment. Click OK to close the dialog box and to see your updated standing in the tournament. You have to click OK again to close that dialog box and move to the tee at the next hole.

Fuji Golf has no timer (golf is supposed to be relaxing, right?). To pause, click Return to Clubhouse under the Game menu. To return to the game after discussing business, politics, and the merits of dry martinis, click Continue Unfinished Round under the picture that appears.

Scoring and Winning

Scoring on the Fuji Golf course is the same as scoring on other golf courses. The number of strokes is totaled at the end of the game and compared to the par for the course. You can see your current score by choosing Score Card from the Options menu. High Scores (which in golf should really be "Low Scores") shows the best finish score and the best tournament finish position. When you first install Fuji Golf, nobody's name appears in this. Whatever your score on the first game, you'll show up in the High Scores chart.

Tips, Traps, and Sneaky Tricks

The best way to improve your game is to mistrust your caddy's choice of clubs. After all, your caddy doesn't have your expertise in the fine art of golf. You may find another club works better for you under certain conditions. And your aim, most assuredly, is always better.

One trick for improving your aim is to use the aerial view to line up the general direction of the shot and then click the pointer on a spot on the horizon of the perspective view, to fine-tune the shot. When you click in the perspective view, a small white line leads out from the club toward the point where you clicked. If you like, you can even drag the line around in either view to get it just right.

Occasionally you may want to share your course with a select group of friends and play a tournament. You can each play a round and then compare your scores in the Tournament Status under the Options menu.

From the keyboard	About the only thing you can do with the keyboard in Fuji Golf is to press F1 for Help. You can also start over pressing F2 or F3 and entering the new name for the score card. This feature doesn't work quite right, however—the views for the holes and the status indicators don't get updated correctly. You'd be better off returning to the clubhouse and then starting a new round.

CHAPTER 20

IdleWild Three

The version of IdleWild in the Entertainment Pack, Volume Three runs exactly the same as the one in Volume Two. The only difference between them is the set of screen savers included with each package. For more information on how to use these screen savers, see the chapters on IdleWild and IdleWild Two in the previous parts of this book, pages 41 and 93.

Volume Three Screen Savers

The IdleWild feature in Microsoft Entertainment Pack Volume Three gives you a choice of eight screen savers. Here's what each does:

Blackness wipes everything from the screen and displays the same black screen you have when your machine is off.

Boat Race is an animated sailboat regatta. The different colored boats appear at the starting line. The race starts and they go out and around the buoys, but there are some inexperienced sailors in this race who occasionally crash into the buoys. After the boats cross the finish line, the first-place boat is awarded a gold cup, the second-place boat gets the silver cup, the third-place winner gets a bronze medal, and the fourth-place skipper is there to show he's not a bad sport.

You have several options with Boat Race. Press F2 to see the Boat Race Options box. Then pick the number of boats and decide how many laps will be in the race. Click on the circle next to the number of boats you want in the race

(1, 2, 4, or random) and next to the number of laps you want the race to run (1, 2, 3, or random).

Chomp An invisible monster takes big bites out of your screen until the screen is empty. The original image then reappears and another random screen saver takes over.

Divide and Conquer splits your screen and displays the entire image in each section. It divides repeatedly until the images all disappear, then randomly selects and runs another screen saver.

The options box (F2) gives you a choice of division methods. Click on the circle next to the type you want.

Fade Away causes your screen image to fade away until the screen is completely blank. Then it picks another screen saver at random and runs it.

IconBownz! blanks your screen, selects an icon and ricochets it off of the sides of your screen. You can use the default icons, or press F2 to select a specific icon. In the dialog box that appears, type the path and filename of an icon file (a .ICO file) or a .EXE file that contains a Windows icon. IconBownz! extracts the icon from the file and displays that the next time it runs.

Oriental Rug blanks the screen and creates a pattern that looks like a Persian carpet. When the image is complete, it starts over again. Use the options (F2) to find a pattern you like.

Tinfoil covers your screen with foil, but almost all of the detail remains. The foil starts at the top of the screen and gradually moves down over the screen image. When the entire image is covered, Tinfoil chooses another screen saver at random and runs it. Tinfoil is one of the coolest of the screen savers. Go ahead and try it. You've got to see the results to be properly impressed.

Trails ...the worms crawl in, the worms crawl out—and they eat everything on your screen. When they've devoured everything in sight, they keep moving across the screen looking for more. These are worms in the archaic sense of the word. They're really snakes. You can set the number of snakes, and the length, width, and craziness of the snakes in the Trails Options dialog box (F2).

Klotski

robably the most challenging game in the Microsoft Entertainment Packs is also the simplest to explain. In its original form, Klotski (Polish for *blocks*) has been delighting Polish children for centuries. It was developed by ZH Computing of Minnesota and Warsaw.

Object of the Game

Klotski began life as a wooden game board that a player could arrange into different puzzles. The object of the original game was to move the blocks around on the game board until a master block could be freed.

The object of the computer version of Klotski is very similar: you move blocks of different sizes and shapes until you can maneuver the red (master) block through an exit and over holes in the playing area, all in the absolute minimum number of moves.

Game Window

Klotski's game window is a large gray field upon which you work one of twenty-four puzzles. The Game menu lets you choose the skill level and the puzzle you want to play.

A puzzle is composed of a number of moveable yellow blocks and one red block, surrounded by a dark blue border with one light blue section. This light blue section is the "gate" through which you must move the red master block.

*"Daisy," puzzle number
1 on level 1*

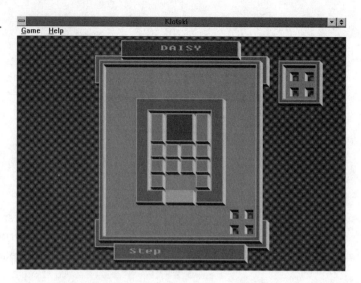

Surrounding the border is a light gray area. A portion of this gray area contains a little "tray" of three-dimensional holes that match the shape of the red block. There is also a small square area with holes big enough to hold the red master block. The name of the puzzle appears at the top of the puzzle, and a display of the number of steps it takes you to solve it is at the bottom.

Play!

Starting the game. Double-click on the Klotski icon in the Entertainment Pack Three group window. A dialog box appears that tells you to choose your game board and wishes you good luck. Click OK.

From the Game menu, choose Level 1, 2, or 3. Level 1 holds simple puzzles, Level 2 gives you not-so-simple puzzles, and Level 3 contains really hard ones. A dialog box appears showing miniature pictures of each of the puzzles in the level you choose. The puzzles are numbered 1 through 8 in approximate order of difficulty. Choose a puzzle by double-clicking on it.

Level 1 selection box

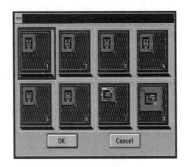

The first time you choose a puzzle, a dialog box appears asking for your name. Enter your name, then click OK. The puzzle you chose appears.

Moves. When you move the pointer over the puzzle, the pointer turns into a hand. Move the blocks by putting the extended finger of the hand on the block you want to move. Then drag the block where you want it to go. You can move the yellow and red blocks anywhere they fit within the boundaries of the puzzle. You can't move any block through the dark blue border.

Move the yellow blocks around until you can move the red block through the light blue gate. Then move the red block into the light gray area around the puzzle. If necessary, move blocks around in the light gray area to get them out of the way, too. Finally, move the red block on top of the tray of holes in the light gray area. The red block "melts" through the holes and appears in the square area off to the right. You get a message from the program telling you how you did and (if appropriate) your name and score are posted on the score chart for the puzzle.

Opening the gate   When the red block is right next to the gate, holes appear in the light blue section. When there are holes in every part of the light blue section, you can open the gate by clicking on the center of the light blue section.

If you'd like to see what all of this looks like, you can choose Demo from the Game menu. A sample puzzle appears, the pointer hand moves down, and the program runs through a typical puzzle solution.

Scoring and Winning

Your score is simply a count of the number of blocks you've moved. Each time you move a block any number of spaces, your score goes up. You win by getting the red block out and over the holes in the tray.

Tips, Traps, and Sneaky Tricks

In general, you should surround the red block with small blocks because, they don't take up a lot of space and are therefore easiest to move.

Once the gate is open, you can move the yellow blocks inside the dark blue border to get them out of the way. You might also need to move the red block over to the gate and open it so you can get some of the obstacle blocks out of your way.

The Open option on the Game menu lets you open other Klotski puzzle files. Klotski is also available as a standalone game that comes with a puzzle editor so you can make your own Klotski puzzles. The standalone version also lets you save and play back partially completed Klotski games, save your moves (so you can recreate your victory and fine-tune it), change colors, and add sound. You can order the standalone version of Klotski, along with a disk of more Klotski puzzles, from ZH Computing, P.O. Box 39764, Edina, MN 55349, (612)432-8461.

From the keyboard   Press F1 for Help. You can also minimize the screen by pressing Esc.

LifeGenesis

ifeGenesis is unique in the Entertainment Pack series, because it contains both a game and a set of mathematical/biological cell-generation simulations that you can just watch and marvel at. It has one of the most interesting histories of anything in the series— definitely worth knowing about.

The Origins of Life

Life began as a mathematical abstraction just over twenty years ago. In 1970, mathematician John Horton Conway wrote the first set of rules for a Life simulation algorithm—a mathematical model of how populations of cells grow and shrink. His three simple rules generated a seemingly endless number of patterns and properties.

But even more amazing was the interest and dedication of the early "Lifers." Lifers were people who were intrigued with the dynamic patterns they could create. Early Lifers worked slowly and carefully on paper or Go boards. As Lifers experimented, they discovered incredible patterns, some of which survive for over 5000 iterations.

Fascination with Life wasn't limited to mathematicians and computer hackers. Articles have appeared in major (and not so major) magazines since the early 1970s, including a 1974 article in *Time*. In 1983, W.H. Freeman and Company published *Wheels, Life, and Other Mathematical*

Amusements, by Martin Gardner. If you're intrigued by Life you may want to get a copy.

LifeGenesis is based on this early work by Conway and others. The next few sections of this chapter explain the Life simulations built in to the LifeGenesis program. In addition to the cell-generation simulations, LifeGenesis has a game you can play against the computer. We'll tell you how it works later, beginning on page 172.

Sit Back and Enjoy Life First

The easiest way to understand life is to just sit back and enjoy it, and that's a good place to start in LifeGenesis. Just remember that you're watching a simulation of the birth, reproduction, and death of biological life forms (*cells*) according to a perfectly logical plan. To begin life, double-click on the LifeGenesis icon in the Entertainment Pack Three group window.

The LifeGenesis window appears as a thirty-by-thirty grid. The squares on the grid are empty because none of the cells is alive yet. Choose Random on the Life menu to create a first generation of cells. Red and blue cells appear on the grid. Now choose Go on the Life menu. Your machine computes generation after generation and displays them, one after another, in the LifeGenesis window. You can sit back and watch the patterns form, change, and either stabilize or disappear. It's amazing to see large areas of cells spring into view or disappear completely, or to watch as an apparently stable area splits apart as another group of cells moves in.

If you want to study each change more closely, make the computer step through each generation as you're ready. Choose Stop on the Life menu or press F6, then choose Next from the Life menu or press F3 when you're ready for the next generation to appear.

Your machine continues to compute generations until all areas are stable. In some cases the stability is manifested as a static set of live cells called a "still life." In others, a

*Standard 30x30
LifeGenesis grid*

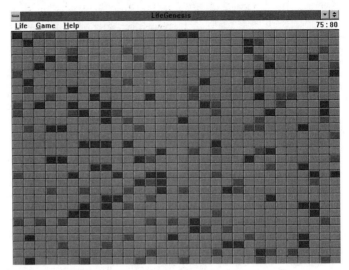

static state occurs where cells are born and die in an oscillating pattern that always reverts to the original configuration after a finite number of iterations.

Over the years, as Lifers have watched Life simulators, they've named certain patterns. Several of the most common ones are included with LifeGenesis. Choose Patterns from the Life menu, then choose one of the patterns from the list that appears. Choose Go from the Life menu and watch what the pattern does.

Understanding Life

Each square on the LifeGenesis grid has eight neighbors: four neighbors next to its sides and four neighbors touching its corners. The fate of every cell on the board is directly related to the condition of its neighboring squares. The rules for cell generation are amazingly simple:

1. A live cell with fewer than two living neighbors dies.
2. A live cell with four or more living neighbors dies.
3. If an empty square has exactly three neighbors containing living cells, it becomes a living cell too.

The corollary for rules 1 and 2 is that a living cell must have two or three living neighbors to stay alive. So just as in real life, neither isolation nor overpopulation is a good condition to sustain life.

LifeGenesis adds a minor modification to rule 3, so that cells can be born either red or blue: a new cell is the same color as the majority of its neighboring cells.

But sometimes the world is flat! Because a computer screen is a finite area, Life programmers have always been faced with the dilemma of what to do about a cell when it reaches the edge of the screen. Sometimes the programmer assumes that the screen wraps around. Thus, cells that travel off the left edge of the screen reappear on the right edge, and vice versa. Other programmers assume that the grid is infinite: although they disappear off the edge, the cells respond as they would if they could just keep on going forever. When cells in LifeGenesis hit the edge of the screen, their pattern changes—cells that fall of the edge of the grid die immediately (Jim Horne calls this "the Columbus effect.") For example, a Glider that normally continues to move across the screen by alternating its pattern becomes a box at the edge of the screen.

The View from Olympus

After you've watched the patterns for a while and feel comfortable with what Life does, you might want to play God. Just as the Greek gods and goddesses watched from Olympus and threw down an occasional thunderbolt to stir things up on earth, you, too, can change life from the Olympus of your office.

Start by redefining the universe. Choose Options from the Life menu. Under Grid in the LifeGenesis Options box, type in a new size for the square grid. It can be as small as five by five or as large as ninety-nine by ninety-nine. But remember that even the Olympians were subject to the laws of nature. If you create a ninety-nine-by-ninety-nine universe and choose Random on the Life menu, Life gets pretty slow (especially in 286 reality). You also get to decide how quickly cell-generation proceeds: in the LifeGenesis

Options box (press F9), slide the button on the Speed bar to slow things down or speed them up.

Throw your thunderbolts into the middle of any of the patterns by adding or deleting cells. To add a cell, click an empty space on the grid. The new cell's color depends on which mouse button you use: the left button adds a blue cell; the right button adds a red one. You can change the color of a living cell by clicking on it with the mouse button for the opposite color. To empty a cell, double-click on it.

Play with the patterns. Let the computer step through the generations as you try to figure out what will happen with each new generation. Create your own life patterns. When you think you've got it all figured out, you're ready to play the LifeGenesis game.

From the keyboard

F1 Help

F3 Next. Begins the next round of cell generation. Use this key after you use F6 (see below).

F5 Go. Start generating cells. Use this key after you've set your options to begin a simulation.

F6 Stop. Pause cell generation. Restart with F3 (see above).

F7 Clear. Clear the grid of cells so you can do something else with it.

F8 Random. Choose a random cell pattern.

F9 Options. Adjust the size of the grid and the speed of each successive generation.

Ctrl-F1 Standard Life Cell Automata. A variant of the LifeGenesis simulations.

Ctrl-F2 Brain Cell Automata. Another variant.

Ctrl-F3 Vote Cell Automata. Yet another variant.

Esc Boss key. Get back to work!

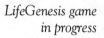

LifeGenesis game
in progress

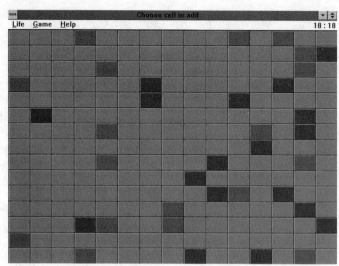

Object of the Game

Now that you understand life a little better, you're ready to try living a little yourself. Your opponent in the LifeGenesis game is your computer. Your objective is to get rid of all the red cells before the computer kills all the blue cells.

Game Window

To start a game, click Game on the menu bar, then choose New game, or press F2. The game opens to a fifteen-by-fifteen grid with an equal number of red and blue cells placed randomly on the board. In the upper-right corner of the game window are two numbers separated by a colon. The number on the left shows how many blue squares are on the board, and the number on the right shows the number of red squares. The pointer is a pencil with the point down.

Across the top of the window, instructions appear directing each move you and the computer make. The first message says, "Choose cell to add." The next message says, "Choose cell to delete." The message "Click to generate" appears when you've completed both your moves.

Play!

Starting the game. Start the LifeGenesis program by double-clicking on the LifeGenesis icon in the Entertainment Pack Three group window. The program opens to the LifeGenesis simulation grid. Choose New Game from the Game menu or press F2. The computer randomly places an equal number of red and blue squares on the board.

Moves. The program gives you and the computer a set sequence of four moves each.

1. You begin by adding a blue cell. The pointer becomes a pencil with the point down. Click on the square where you want to add a blue cell.

2. Now it's time to delete a red cell. The pointer becomes a pencil with the eraser down. Click on the red cell you want to delete. (Don't worry yet about strategy. Just learn the drill first.)

3. Next, click anywhere to begin the generation process. The pattern of red and blue cells changes once. This means the program has executed one cycle of the cell-generation sequence. The ratio in the upper-right corner of the game window reflects the change, with your score on the left and the computer's score on the right.

4. Finally, click anywhere again to give the computer its turn.

These are the mechanics of LifeGenesis's legal moves. The hard part is deciding where to add and delete blue and red cells. Review the rules of LifeGenesis on page 169. Then study the grid for the best place to add a blue cell. You want to place a blue cell so that it will mate with its neighbors to generate more blue cells. Next, find a red cell that's supporting its neighbors in a stable pattern, or one that's getting ready to multiply. Remember, you don't need to worry about areas that have a lot of red cells. These will clear out from over-population.

After you click to generate the results of adding and deleting cells, the pointer turns into an icon of a two-button mouse and stays that way until you click either mouse button anywhere in the game window. Now the computer makes its moves. It adds a red cell, deletes a blue cell, and computes the next life generation. When the pointer goes back to being a pencil, it's your turn again. You and the computer alternate turns until either all the red cells are gone and you win or all the blue cells are gone and you lose.

You can click either the left or the right mouse button for any action while playing the game of LifeGenesis. If you try to make an illegal move, you get a message that says "Choose a red cell to delete" or "You can only add to an empty square."

Skill levels. Use the Game menu to choose a skill level, from Easy, through Hard, to Very Hard. On the Easy level, the computer's moves are completely random. Any good moves it makes are just luck. On the Hard level, the computer looks at each blank cell, determines what would happen if it added a cell there, and then tries the next until it finds the cell that will create the most red cells and kill the most blue cells to give it the biggest lead. The computer then does the same thing to figure out which of your cells to delete. On the Very Hard level, the computer tries every possible combination of adds and deletes on the grid to see which works out the best for it. This may take a while on a slower computer.

Also, on the Easy and Hard levels, the computer randomly sets only eighteen squares to red and eighteen

From the keyboard	You can't play LifeGenesis from the keyboard, but there are some accelerator keys to speed things up.
F1	Help
F2	New Game
Alt-F10	Hint.

squares to blue. On the Very Hard level, the computer randomly sets twenty-one red and twenty-one blue squares.

Endgame. You can quit a game any time by choosing Quit this game from the Game menu. To play another round, choose New Game from the Game menu or press F2.

Scoring and Winning

In the upper-right corner, the computer tracks how many blue cells and how many red cells remain on the board after each cycle of moves. The number on the left represents blue cells and the number on the right represents the red. The computer keeps count during the game, but you don't actually score in the game of life, you just win or lose.

You win when all of the red cells are wiped out. You're awarded the Nobel Prize Science Medal in the LifeGenesis Game Over box, along with the message "Congratulations, you win!" Click on OK in the dialog box; the computer displays the original life-simulation plane.

Tips, Traps, and Sneaky Tricks

You've got the edge in Life. Because you always get the first move, you have a better chance to win than the computer has. Study the board. You can ignore all of the areas with only one or two red cells, and all the areas that are heavily populated by red cells, because they are going to die immediately. Look for areas with three or four cells. Remember, only cells with two or three neighbors live. Try to add a blue cell that gives as many other blue cells as possible a chance to live. Then try to find a red cell to delete that will take away the life support of other red cells.

You also have an advantage over the computer because it doesn't bother to develop a long-term strategy. Watch the moves it makes; sometimes it can be pretty smart, but if you plan ahead, you can beat it.

To assure yourself an easy win, use the Hint option on the Game menu all the way through. When it's your turn

Life patterns

Traffic Lights   starts as a row of five cells and ends as four blinking traffic lights. (Okay, so you have to use your imagination!)

Honey Farm   starts as seven cells in a row and becomes four hives.

Oscillators   always return to their original pattern after several generations.

Pulsar   is one of the most beautiful of the patterns displayed. It starts as a very simple line with two live cells below it, one at each end. It then splits into two mirrored patterns, then splits again into four. It finally settles into three patterns.

Gliders   are Oscillators that return to their original shape after four generations, but they move diagonally one square in the process. Run Gliders to see the edge effect (which is discussed later in this chapter): when the pattern has run its course, two square, four-cell still lifes (called "boxes") rest against opposite corners.

Spaceships   are like Gliders, but they fly straight instead of diagonally.

Eaters   are amazing creatures, kind of the "Audrey Two" of the computer world. They can swallow Gliders and Spaceships and not change themselves. (This one is really worth seeing—try it!).

Virus   shows how a single cell can upset multiple stable still lifes.

The Glider Gun   produces Gliders. It is an Oscillator, but each time it returns to its original configuration, it shoots off a Glider. The Eater in the lower-left part of the window eats the Gliders as they come in.

to add a cell (at the very beginning of the game), press Alt-F10. The pencil point (the pointer) jumps to the "hinted" square. Click the mouse, being *very* careful not to move it as you do. Repeat this process to delete one of the red cells. Then click once to begin the generating process and once more to give the computer its turn. Continue this cycle until the game ends. At the Easy and Hard skill levels you'll win very quickly. At the Very Hard level, you'll still win, but it takes longer.

Variations on the theme of life. There's another game you can play in LifeGenesis. Generate a random pattern by pressing F5, then try to destroy every live cell by adding new cells. Here's an example: add a cell in the center of the Traffic Lights pattern. You win if you clear the grid of all the cells; you lose if the pattern stops and becomes stable.

There's a deeper meaning to life if you know its hidden mysteries, and Jim Horne, the author of LifeGenesis, has shared some with you. The following paragraphs tell you how to run cell-generation simulations based on variations of the three standard LifeGenesis rules.

John Conway's rules for life are an example of cellular automata. While his rules are the most popular, many others exist. Two other sets of rules are hidden away in LifeGenesis. You can access them if you know the right hidden keys, which are described in the following sections.

When you're through experimenting with these alternate life-forms, return to standard LifeGenesis cell-generation simulations by pressing Ctrl-F1. If you start a game from the Game menu, the program returns to the standard LifeGenesis cell-generation rules automatically.

Brain Cell Automata. Ctrl-F2 sets LifeGenesis to the Brain Cell Automata variant (so called because the patterns it develops resemble the lines on a brain) of the LifeGenesis cell-generation simulation. Brain's rules are slightly different from the standard LifeGenesis rules, and are based on the two colors available in LifeGenesis. The cells in this variant multiply very quickly. If you put just two cells next to each other in the middle of a grid, they grow to fill almost the entire grid. Like standard LifeGenesis, Brain is based on three rules:

1. A blue cell turns red on the next generation.
2. A red cell empties on the next generation.
3. An empty cell with exactly two neighbors turns blue.

Vote Cell Automata. Ctrl-F3 sets LifeGenesis to Vote Cell Automata, a one-color system of cell-generation simulation that tends to shrink. If you populate your screen by choosing Random from the Life menu and then run Vote, the screen clears very quickly. At best you may end up with a few four-cell boxes or a simple Oscillator. But Vote gives you one of the most interesting effects in Life-Genesis: press F8 several times to populate the grid with lots of cells, and then press F5 to start the cell-generation process. In one or two generations, you get a life form that looks like a single large, pulsating blue cell. It slowly shrinks, but it's interesting to watch. Vote has two rules:

1. Colors are not considered in Vote. A cell is either alive or dead.

2. The fate of each cell, alive or dead, depends on a vote of its neighbors. All neighbors and the cell itself vote with their own value (zero if a neighbor is dead, one if alive). The votes are then tallied. If the majority votes one, the cell lives; otherwise, it dies. Unfortunately, the cells live in a sleazy electoral jurisdiction, and all five-to-four votes are overturned.

The corollary to rule 2: If a cell has more than five neighbors or exactly three neighbors plus itself, it is alive in the next generation. If not, it is dead.

CHAPTER 23

SkiFree

 kiFree is your chance to take a little break from work and hit the slopes, even in July. There you are with your parka and ski boots, zipping down the slope at breakneck speed, jumping moguls, scaring the novices, and (wham!) crashing into trees. You're busy racking up points for speed and style.

SkiFree started out as a very simple entertainment from Chris Pirih. You just skied down the hill forever. There weren't any statistics, no scores, no timer. It was rather pleasant. But co-workers at Microsoft wanted this feature and that feature, and a way to keep score, and a timer, and pretty soon, it became a real game.

Object of the Game

The joy of SkiFree is to just bomb down the slope having fun. Just like real skiing, there's no particular reason to play except to goof off. If you're a competitive type, you can try your hand moving up in the rankings in the style and speed categories. There are even hazards on the course: snowboarders, novices, dogs, and Abominable Snowmen!

Game Window

The game opens to the top of a ski slope with your skier (that's you), some signs, and a chair lift complete with other skiers. There's also a box in the top-right corner of the window that shows your time, distance, speed, and style

Opening SkiFree window

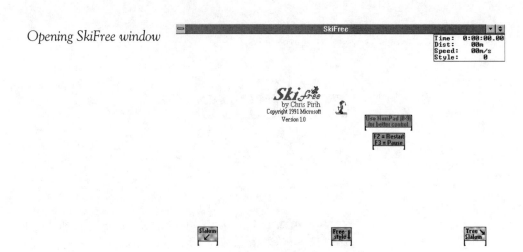

points. From the top, you can go down the Slalom, Free-style, or Tree Slalom runs depending on whether you want to bomb down the mountain on a Slalom run, getting points for elapsed time, or whether you want points for style on the Free-style run. You can even skip all three runs and just mess around if you don't feel like being competitive.

Mouse or keyboard?

Free-Style SkiFree plays much better with the keyboard than with the mouse. The keyboard gives you greater control and options that simply aren't possible with the mouse. On the other hand, the mouse gives you more fluid control by letting you change direction quicker. The slaloms are a lot easier with the mouse, where you can develop a smooth side-to-side movement that lets you *schuss* gracefully by the markers. Try both ways and see which you prefer.

Press F2 to start a new game. Press F3 to pause the game. Press Esc to leave the slopes and return to your office. You can't press F1 to get Help for a good reason: there isn't any. In fact, there aren't any menus at all!

*Right above
the starting flags*

Play!

Starting the game. The game begins as soon as you double-click the SkiFree icon in the Entertainment Pack Three group window. You're waiting at the top of the hill. Control your movements down the hill by using the mouse or the arrow keys on the keyboard.

Moves. Press the left or right arrows to move to the left or right. Press the down arrow to go down the slope. Press the up arrow key to sidestep up the mountain. Pressing the Home or PgUp keys faces you to the left or the right. You can then ski horizontally across the mountain by holding down the left or right arrow key. To use the mouse, you move the pointer with the mouse in the direction that you want to go. Both the mouse and the keyboard let you steer in 30-degree increments.

Start down a course by maneuvering to the two starting flags at the 37-meter mark and skiing through them. There are three pairs of flags marking the start of each course. Be careful to go through the pair of flags that are pointing toward each other. If you go through the flags that mark either side of a course, you won't rack up any points. Of course, if you just feel like messing around, skip the gates entirely and head downhill.

Bang! The gun sounds and you're off! Now what?

Obstacles and hazards. Apart from the slalom runs having red and blue markers for the course (which you'll read about in a moment), all three runs look pretty much alike. As you plunge down the mountain, you see trees and stumps, rocks, moguls, ski jumps, snowplowing novices, dogs, and occasional monsters with potbellies. Some you'll avoid and some you can't, some you'll aim for, and some you'll just want to mess with.

Most of what you're avoiding are the trees. Trees come in a bunch of sizes and shapes, but none of them will get out of your way, so ski around them. You also want to avoid the rocks (gray bumps) and the stumps (brown bumps with flat tops), all of which make you crash if you run into them. You can ski around these or just jump over them. Moguls are white, bumpy outlines and are good to avoid or jump because they slow you down.

Snowboarders don't look out for you—you have to look out for them. Snowboarders knock you over while they fly down the mountain still grinning. (You get to do this back to them and to the novices, besides, so it all evens out.) Speaking of novices, you can knock them into the snow by skiing closely right by them, but if you get too close you crash into them. Dogs on the course go "Woof!" when you do this to them.

If you run squarely into any obstacle, you crash and say "Ouch!" You can jump over a lot of the smaller obstacles if there's a conveniently placed mogul or a ski jump (a rainbow-striped horizontal bar).

Slaloms. Both Slalom and Tree Slalom courses have red and blue markers. You need to run around the markers, just like in regular slalom skiing. If you go around the gate on the correct side it turns to a green happy face. Going around the gate on the wrong side turns it to a red sad face.

Free-style. Free-styling down the mountain is not just a matter of dodging trees and scaring novices, but that's a darn good start. A good rule of thumb when free-styling is that if it looks like fun or is silly, it probably earns you points. If it looks like it's painful, you usually lose points.

Once you've jumped over something and are in the air, you can do a lot of different fancy jumps. To do a helicopter (sort a pirouette in midair), press either the left or right arrow, or spin the pointer around the skier. To do a head-over-heels flip, press the up or down arrow, or click the mouse. The more times you press the up or down arrow or click the mouse, the more times you flip. The fanciest jump you can do is a "backscratcher," where you bend your knees so your skis touch your back. Start by doing a helicopter and then press the up arrow. Pressing the down arrow gets you out of the backscratcher.

Whenever you come out of a jump, try to land smoothly. You lose points for crashing; besides which, it's ungraceful.

Endgame. By the 1040-meter mark, all three courses have ended. Most people just keep skiing down the hill. Sounds good, no? Well, as SkiFree was being developed, it turned out there was a bug in the software: after a while, the statistics went negative because of an overflow condition somewhere in the program.

There are two ways to fix a bug like this. One is to find out exactly why the number is going negative and stop it, the other is to install a "trap" that prevents the conditions that cause the bug from happening. In other words, you can treat the disease or treat the symptoms.

Enter the Abominable Snowmen. The numbers went negative whenever the skier went too far down, up, or to either side. Chris Pirih put in four Abominable Snowmen at the corners of a rectangle 2000 meters down the hill, 128 meters up the hill (you herringbone up from the starting position), or 1000 meters to either side. If you go past any one of the sides of the rectangle, an Abominable Snowman dashes out and eats you. It then jumps up and down, yells

Snowman and upcoming lunch

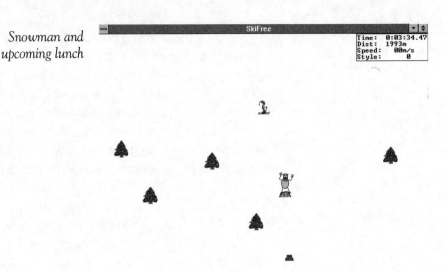

at you, and waves its skinny little arms. The thing that causes the numbers to go negative has been effectively trapped: the game is over and you must exit and restart to do anything else. Here's a picture of the Abominable Snowman right before eating lunch. His unsuspecting meal sits at the 1993-meter mark.

And that, ladies and gentlemen, is how you do a code trap with style.

SkiFree is unique in that it has no menus whatsoever. To exit SkiFree, you need to double-click the Control bar in the upper-left corner of the window.

Abominable things you should know

If you move directly below, above, or to either side of the starting area and just inside the rectangle, you can see the Abominable Snowman before it eats you.

If you go out right at the corner of the rectangle, you might get two Abominable Snowmen at once. Unfortunately, they don't eat each other; they just eat skiers.

You don't lose points for getting eaten, but it's no great honor, either.

Scoring and Winning

Scores for all three events appear in a dialog box when you reach the end of the course. Close the dialog box by clicking OK. You can keep skiing down the hill, although it doesn't affect your score.

Slaloms. Scoring the slaloms is simple. Your base score is the time it takes you to go from Start at the 37-meter mark to either the 540-meter mark in the Slalom or the 1040-meter mark in the Tree Slalom. You lose five seconds for each slalom you miss on the course.

Free-style. As you bomb down the Free-Style run, you earn style points between the 37-meter mark and the 1040-meter mark. Having no fear is a plus to amassing style points for antics such as jumps, trick skiing, and trick skiing off the jumps. One of the advantages to SkiFree is that you can land on your head after a 100-meter jump and not even walk funny. After the dialog box appears, you can just goof off the rest of the way down—style points are only earned on the course.

There are a lot of things you can earn and lose style points for in Free-Style:

	POINTS	
ACTION	EARN	LOSE
Scaring a dog	3	
Jumping over anything	6	
Making a novice crash	20	
Making a snowboarder crash	20	
Jumping over a magic mushroom	100	
Jumping over a burning tree	1000	
Crashing into an obstacle		32
Going over yellow snow		16
Crash landing		64

ACTION	POINTS
Doing a backscratcher	Earn a number of points equal to eight times the amount of time you're in the air (as measured in some really arbitrary small time unit.)
Doing a head-over-heels flip	Earn a number of points equal to four times the amount of time you're in the air.
Doing a helicopter	Earn a number of points equal to twice the amount of time you're in the air.
Just being in the air	Earn a number of points equal to the amount of time you're in the air.

Tips, Traps, and Sneaky Tricks

SkiFree has more hidden features and options than any other game in the Microsoft Entertainment Packs. Most of the neat features are aimed at the free-stylers, but there's fun stuff for every type of skier.

Game not moving fast enough for you? Press the letter F to switch to "fast" mode. You'll move about twice as fast, making it that much more painful when you splat into a tree. Press F again to return to "slow" mode.

Don't back up too far to get a running start at trees, rocks, or ski jumps. These are placed randomly on the hill only when they need to be—which is to say, SkiFree doesn't worry about where things are until they're just about to show up on the screen. (Note, however, that Slaloms and the ski lift are always where you expect them, even if you can't see them.) If you move up the hill to get a good long run at a ski jump and the ski jump goes off the bottom of the screen, it probably won't be there when you come blazing down the hill at it. You may find instead that there's nothing, a mogul, or perhaps a big, friendly tree to play with at 90 miles an hour.

If you scare a dog, it usually says "Woof!" Occasionally, though, you *really* scare a dog, which results in yellow snow. Don't ski over the yellow snow; you lose 16 style points.

You usually want to avoid hitting trees, but in one case, it's worth your while. If you jump and hit a dead tree in midair, it catches fire. If you then walk up the hill and jump over it while it's burning, you get 1000 style points.

If you find a tree stump and walk uphill over it, it turns into a mushroom. You get 100 style points if you then jump over it. You'll know that you were successful because the mushroom disappears.

So many people asked Chris Pirih if there was a way to avoid the Abominable Snowmen that he put one in at the last minute. If you take a good jump in "fast" mode right before going past the 2000-meter mark going straight downhill, you see an Abominable Snowman running beside you trying to catch you. (You'll also see the number in the statistics box go negative; the bug is still there and by outrunning the Abominable Snowman, the condition hasn't been trapped.) Look out for obstacles and don't crash. Sooner or later, the map for SkiFree wraps around, and you find yourself at the start gates for the second time... and the Abominable Snowman can't chase you inside the game area. You did it! Take a moment to catch your breath, and you're ready to head down the slopes again.

CHAPTER 24

TetraVex

etraVex is a simple little puzzle. All you have to do is arrange tiles in a grid in such a way that each of the four characters on each of the tiles' sides matches the characters on the sides of all its neighboring tiles. Sounds easy, right? It is, until you increase the number of tiles in the grid. Lots of hair-pulling, teeth-grinding fun.

Scott Ferguson wrote Tetravex in response to a mathematical conundrum that had held his interest for some time: how do you tile an infinite plane using four-sided tiles? Solving this problem, he noticed, was something like playing dominoes. What started as a mildly engaging geometric exercise eventually became a challenging game in the Microsoft Entertainment Pack, Volume Three.

Object of the Game

To win at TetraVex, you have to figure out how to arrange a set of tiles on a grid so that the characters on all the adjacent edges of each piece match. Like a good host, the game quietly and casually ejects any tile from the grid if it doesn't fit in. You win if you get all the tiles onto the grid.

Game Window

The TetraVex game window is dominated by a gray grid "tray," in which you're supposed to arrange tiles. Off to the right are just enough tiles to fill the tray. (The tiles and the tray are great examples of three-dimensional graphics when displayed on a VGA monitor.) The characters on the tiles start out as numbers, but you can choose letters, Greek characters, or even symbols if you like. If you want to play a timed game, a timer appears above the grid tray.

3x3 default layout in TetraVex

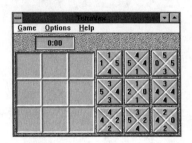

Play!

Starting the game. Start TetraVex by double-clicking the TetraVex icon in the Entertainment Pack Three group window. When you start TetraVex for the first time, the grid you have to solve is three squares on a side, and the game is timed. A timed game starts as soon as the game window appears, so be ready to go. If you don't see the Timer box above the grid and you want to record your scores, choose Timer from the Options menu. (This restarts the game if you're in the middle of one.)

Moves. To move a tile to the tray, put the pointer on the tile and drag it where you want it to go. If one of the sides doesn't match its neighbor, the piece floats back to the right of the tray. You can also reposition the pieces already in the tray by dragging them.

If you think you know exactly where a tile goes and you don't want to move it again by accident, bolt it down by double-clicking it in the tray. A bolt-head appears in the middle of the tile. If you discover that you made a mistake and the tile really should be somewhere else, unbolt the tile by double-clicking on it again. The bolt-head vanishes. You can then move the tile and even bolt it down again if you feel like it.

*3x3 game in progress
with tiles bolted down*

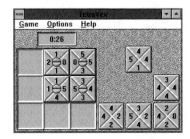

If you get completely stuck, get a hint by choosing Hint from the Game menu, or just pressing Ctrl-H. TetraVex moves a single tile to its proper position in the tray and bolts it down. When you just can't take it anymore, solve the rest of the game by choosing Solve from the Game menu or pressing Ctrl-S. All the tiles move to the appropriate places in the tray. Any tiles that weren't in the right place are repositioned. Stop TetraVex in mid-solve by pressing Ctrl-S again, then pick up the game from there.

Options. TetraVex lets you customize the game a couple of ways. Play TetraVex as an untimed game (a good practice while you're learning) by clicking on Timer in the Options menu. (A checkmark appears next to an option when it's turned on.)

Skill levels. TetraVex gives you two ways to make the game tougher as you improve. You can change the number of tiles in the puzzle, or the number of characters in the tile set.

TetraVex defaults to a three-by-three grid, which gives you only nine tiles to fit into the tray. That's really much too easy for most of you. Choose Size from the Options menu to change this to a grid from two by two through six

From the keyboard

Press F1 for help. Press F2 to start a new game. Press F3 to pause the game. Press Ctrl-H for a hint. Press Ctrl-S to solve the game. Press Esc to minimize the game and pretend you were really doing something important.

by six. The six-by-six game should keep you off the streets for hours.

Choose Digits from the Options menu to pick the number of digits, letters, or symbols to be used in the tile set. The default is ten, which means that the numerals 0 through 9, letters A through J, or Greek characters α through φ appear on the tiles. If you only have six digits on the tiles, you only see numbers 0 through 5, letters A through F, or Greek characters α through φ on the tiles. The more digits you have on the tiles, the easier it is to solve the puzzle.

Endgame. When you've successfully placed all the tiles, a big yellow happy face appears to let you know you've won. If your score qualifies, you also get to put your name in the High Score table. You can play again by clicking New Game under the Game menu, clicking on the happy face, or pressing F2.

If you got a hint during the game, when you finish you just get a tepid smirk on the happy face, rather than the great big grin you get if you did it all by yourself. If you solve the puzzle with the Solve option, the timer continues to run until you unbolt a tile, move it off the grid, then drop it back into place again as if you were solving the thing yourself. You then get the same lukewarm smile when you finish as you did with the hint.

Digits in TetraVex aren't just numbers

You can choose Numbers, Letters, or Greek characters from the Options menu to set the characters you want to appear on the tiles. The default is Numbers, but you should try a couple games with Letters and Greek just to see what they're like. If you have the Zapf Dingbats font on your computer, you can also choose Symbols from the Options menu, for a change of pace.

3x3 screen with really happy face

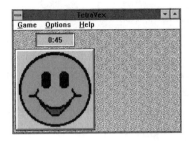

Scoring and Winning

TetraVex doesn't record scores unless you play with the timer on. If you got a hint or used Solve to solve the game, you won't see a score for the game—after all, fair is fair.

TetraVex calculates your score according to how long it takes you to finish the puzzle and how hard the puzzle was. If you're not playing with the timer you can sit back and relax. There's no hurry because no score is recorded.

Tips, Traps, and Sneaky Tricks

When you first start, play smaller puzzles to get the feel of the game. Try a few two-by-two games to see what moving and bolting tiles is like. Then try some three-by-three games. When you get better at it, move to the bigger challenges of four-by-four and five-by-five grids. Don't try the six by six 'til you're really confident. TetraVex author Scott Ferguson admits he hasn't solved one of those yet.

Before you start moving tiles in a puzzle (particularly the larger ones), see if any have edges that don't match any other piece. These certainly belong on one of the borders. For instance, if a tile has a 6 on the top but there isn't another tile with a 6 on the bottom, you know that the 6-on-the-top tile goes somewhere along the top row. Once you have the first piece positioned on a border, the other pieces are much easier to fit around it.

You can reposition a whole group of matching tiles in the tray by right-clicking and dragging them. You can also bolt down or unbolt a group of tiles by right-double-clicking the group. Remember, moving or bolting down a whole group of tiles doesn't mean that they're in the right places in the tray, just that they all fit together.

Make the TetraVex window fill your whole screen by clicking the top-left button on the game window and choosing Maximize from the menu. The tray and the tiles take up a relatively small space when you Maximize, which gives you room to move some of the tiles off to other parts of the screen. This lets you separate and build up groups of tiles that go together. When you think you know where a tile or group goes, put it in the tray and bolt it down.

When you use the open space in the window as a workspace, it may get pretty messy. When this happens, rearrange the tiles by choosing Arrange from the Game menu. This puts all the tiles on the workspace back into nice neat rows next to the tray. You can also use the Arrange command to give you a new perspective on the tiles occasionally. You might see a combination of tiles that you overlooked before. Be careful, though—the Arrange command doesn't put things back in any particular order.

If you're thinking you can pause the game to buy some time while you solve the puzzle, forget it. Choosing Pause from the Game menu or pressing F3 blanks out the grid and erases the tiles. (Gee, you'd think that Scott thought people were going to cheat or something.) To start the game again, click Resume on the Game menu or press F3 again. (You can't pause a game that doesn't have the timer running.)

There's only one way to cheat at TetraVex. When you get a hint or run the game with the Solve command, hold down the Shift key the whole time the pieces are moving. Then, when you move the last piece into place, you see the happy face with the big smile and also get to enter your name on the high scores table, just as if you'd done the whole thing yourself. There's one exception to this stunt. When you solve the six-by-six puzzle, either by yourself or with the help of the Shift key, you don't see a happy face. Instead, you see a familiar green symbol from Microsoft's past. Check it out for yourself.

TriPeaks

s you scan the horizon from left to right you see spread before you in all their glory Peak Ahmadas, Peak Gehaldi, and Peak Zackheer. You ask yourself why you're taking on such a risky mission, but the answer is simple—money. You get money—lots of it—by scaling these treacherous peaks one card at a time.

TriPeaks, the last of the solitaire card games in the Entertainment Packs, is Robert Hogue's first Windows program. When Robert got tired of playing the Solitaire game that comes with Windows, he wanted to invent a new one of his own, so he bought a book of solitaire card games for inspiration. But none of the games in the book really seemed to have the right flavor. So, Robert combined his favorite features from the best games in the book into a new game, which he dubbed TriPeaks. The names of the mountain peaks are made up. Earlier versions of TriPeaks used names like Everest and Rainier, but they just didn't sound exotic enough. These are a little more "religious" sounding—real spiritual mountain names.

TriPeaks is different from the other card games in the Entertainment Packs in that it can accumulate and record lifetime scores. Another difference is that all the other card games are designed to take time. Robert designed TriPeaks to be quick, something for fun when you only have only a minute or two to squeeze in a game ... sort of the Entertainment Pack equivalent of a cocktail peanut.

Opening TriPeaks layout

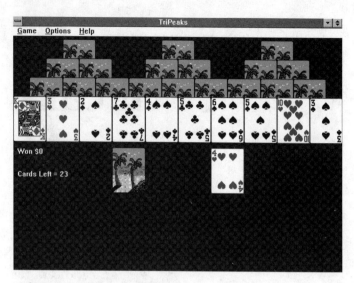

Object of the Game

From the initial TriPeaks tableau, you build runs with cards one higher or one lower in rank than the top card on the discard pile (similar to Golf from the Microsoft Entertainment Pack, Volume One). You earn dollars for each card in a run, and bonus money, too. Big bucks are the goal here. You don't need to clear the tableau to cash in substantially—but it does help.

Game Window

The TriPeaks tableau is in the top half of the window. The bottom half contains the stock, the discard pile, and (optionally) the statistics bar. Your current winnings (or losses) and a tally of the number of cards left in the stock appear in the lower-left part of the window.

Play!

Starting the game. Start the game by double-clicking the TriPeaks icon in the Entertainment Pack Three group window. The green TriPeaks "card table" appears, along with a dialog box asking you for your name. Enter your gambling alias, to keep track of your winnings; then click OK. Your score starts at $0. To begin playing, choose Deal from the Game menu or press F2. TriPeaks deals the cards to the tableau and turns up one card to the discard pile. This is the first card of your run.

Moves. The idea in TriPeaks is to play as long a run as possible from the exposed cards in the tableau to the top card of the discard pile. In this game, a run is a sequence of cards in ascending rank, descending rank, or both. For instance, a valid run could be 4-3-2-3-4-5. Cards in the runs can be any suit and any color. TriPeaks even lets you "wrap around" a run—play an ace on a king, or a king on an ace, then a queen, and so on. Move a card from the tableau to the discard pile by clicking on the card you want to move. (For definitions of card game terms and rank values, see the chapter on Solitaire, page 18 of this book.)

Let's use the layout in the first figure, to illustrate. You can play a pretty good run starting with the 4 on the discard pile: 4-3-2-3-4-5-6-7. Start by clicking on the 3 and then the 2 at the left end of the bottom row of the tableau, followed by the other 3. All three cards flip in sequence to the discard pile.

Although you're going to take both 3's off the board, you should always expose the cards hidden in the three peaks as soon as you can. It may make a difference to your strategy. As soon as a hidden card is freed, it flips over. In this case, you reveal a 7—might be interesting if some other cards come up, but nothing special right now.

Now take the 4-5-6-7 from the center of the tableau. Again, take the 5 next to the 4 instead of the 5 further to the right, so you expose one more card. Removing 4-5-6 reveals a jack (no help) and another 6. Hmmm, perhaps you can use that new 6 with the 7 for two additional cards in the run. Playing the 7 reveals another 4.

The new 4 changes your strategy: rather than add 6-7 to your run for two more cards, you can play 6-5-4 for three more cards. Careful playing gave you three extra cards! The

*In the middle
of the first run*

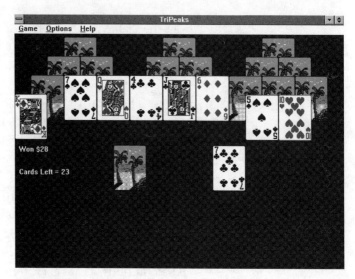

completed run has used up 11 cards, netted you $55, and
opened the tableau up nicely.

Continuing to play this hand, you click on the stock.
The next card in the discard pile is a 2 (no help), so click
on the stock again. The next card is an ace—a very good
card indeed! Play A-K-Q-J-10. Start by playing the king on
the left to reveal the card underneath—which turns out to
be another ace! You're in luck. Play the ace and then play
the other king, followed by Q-J-10. Your luck is still hold-

After the first run

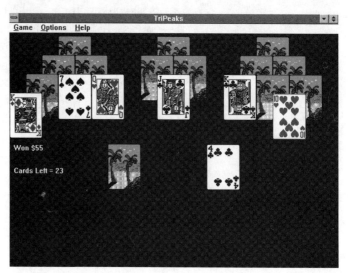

After the second run

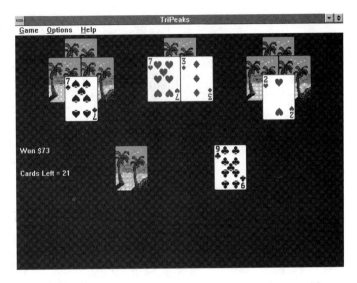

ing; the 10 reveals a 2 and a 9. Click on the 9 to add it to the run. The final run becomes A-K-A-K-Q-J-10-9, and leaves the tableau as shown here.

Keep going with this hand until you either clear the tableau or run out of cards in the stock.

Options. Tripeaks gives you three options that don't really affect the way the game works, but they're kinda fun.

A new deck from the dealer. Choose Deck from the Options menu. TriPeaks gives you eight dazzling new

From the keyboard

TriPeaks has a complete set of keyboard keys, and is a good game to play on a laptop while you're waiting in a crowded doctor's office. Press F1 for help and F2 to start a new game. Use the left and right arrow keys to position the pointer over a card. To move the card, press Enter. To play another card from the stock, press the down arrow key to move the pointer to the stock and then press Enter. To move the pointer back up to the tableau, press the up arrow key. (You can use either the arrow keys on the numeric keypad or on the T-shaped arrow keypad.) Minimize the game by pressing Esc.

choices of card backs to choose from. Avid Microsoft games players will recognize versions of the fish, the roses, the haunted castle, and San Felipe (sorry, the last two aren't animated in this incarnation). There are four new designs, one of which is the three mountain peaks, Ahmadas, Gehaldi, and Zackheer. Double-click the card back you want. If you're playing without a mouse, choose a deck by pressing the left and right arrow keys to highlight your choice; then press Enter.

Getting the stats. The statistics bar doesn't appear when you first install and run TriPeaks, but you can add it by choosing Show Statistics from the Options menu. The Statistics bar gives you more info than you'll ever need. See the sidebar for details.

The Hall of Fame. Choose Hall of Fame from the Options menu to bring up a list of former TriPeaks champions. Compare your score against theirs. How do you stack up, big spender?

Changing players. Play tournament-style by setting up a whole squad of individual player names. Then play a set number of games. To do this, choose Change Player from the Game menu and enter a new name. TriPeaks adds the name to the scoreboard. Then take turns, using the Change Player option to switch back and forth between players. Different strategies may also call for different identities: you

The Statistics Bar

The statistics bar shows a lot of information:

- the winnings for this game and this session
- the number of games played this session by this player
- the most won and lost in any game
- the average winnings or losses for the session
- the average winnings or losses for this player
- the value of the current streak
- the total number of games this session
- the longest streak and what it was worth

can experiment with other ways of playing by setting up aliases for yourself.

Endgame. This game doesn't really end. It's kind of like playing in Reno—you stop when your judgment tells you you'd better. A *hand* ends when you clear all three peaks of cards or when you run out of cards in the stock.

To start a new hand, choose Deal from the Game menu or press F2. If you start a new hand before you finish the current one, you're assessed a whopping penalty. Think twice. The computer says, "You are trying to redeal with cards left in play for a penalty of *x* dollars. Do you really want to redeal?" The penalty is equal to five times the number of cards left in the tableau, so it's often substantial. At this point you've probably changed your mind, so click the No button and finish the current hand.

To exit TriPeaks, double-click on the gray button at the top-left corner of the game window. If you're in the middle of a hand, the computer says, "You are exiting with cards left in play for a penalty of *x* dollars. —OUCH!! Do you really want to quit?" Again, the dollar amount of the penalty is five times the number of cards languishing in the tableau. Click Yes if money means nothing to you.

If all the cards in the stock are gone, you can start a new game or exit TriPeaks without suffering a penalty.

Scoring and Winning

Scoring is cumulative, over as many hands and as many sessions as you want to play. The game remembers the score of each player registered, even after you exit TriPeaks. Your

| **Next stop, Monte Carlo** | Game author Robert Hogue has played more than 6000 games in the last year. His best score was $259, and his longest streak was twenty-one cards. He's about to break $100,000. He adds that he knows of twenty-one people who are over $10,000 and five who are over $50,000. |

actual score is based on how many cards you play in each run. The first card is worth $1, the second, $2, and so on. The longer the run, the higher your score. This is how you make most of your money.

TriPeaks pays bonuses for superlative performance. When you reach the summit of the first two peaks, you get a $15 bonus to urge you forward to the final ascent. When you reach the third summit, you're rewarded with a $30 bonus. The most you get for any one game is $406. This is for a perfect run of all the cards in the tableau on the first card in the discard pile. Good luck!

TriPeaks takes money back in some cases. Every time you play a card from the stock, you're charged $5. If you quit while there are still cards in the tableau and in the stock, you're charged $5 for each card left on the tableau.

If you've played TriPeaks before, you'll see a dollar figure in the space after the "won," under the tableau when you reload the game. If you want to declare bankruptcy and start over, click Reset on the Game menu. A dialog box appears and asks if you're sure you want to wipe out your winnings and start over. If you click on Yes, the card table clears and the dollar figure in the "won" space reverts to $0.

Tips, Traps, and Sneaky Tricks

The key to winning big at this table is to set up long runs. The more cards you play in a single run, the more money you win. Take your time planning your runs—TriPeaks has no timer. Also remember that you can't Undo a move in this game—if you click on the wrong legal card, you're stuck with it. A card laid is a card played. (If you click on a card that isn't legal, nothing happens.)

If you just play the game casually, you tend to break even or win a little. To really clobber the score, pay attention to the cards that have appeared. For example, if you've already played all but one of the 4's and 6's, a 5 could really slow you down. Similarly, going through all the 5's at the beginning of a game forms a roadblock. When you later play a 6 or a 4, you haven't as many options for making runs. Counting your cards might also let you know that there are still four 8's and three 10's lurking in the stock, which could be Worth Knowing late in the game.

TriPeaks author Robert Hogue says that most people make the same mistake: they just start playing without finding out how to win the game. If you try to clear all three peaks every time, you won't win big. If there are half a dozen cards left on the tableau, one of the peaks has already been removed, and perhaps a dozen cards left in the stock, consider quitting and taking the penalty. Here's why: the most you can make by removing the cards on the tableau in a single run is $21 for the six cards in the run, plus $15 for the second peak, and $30 for the last peak, for a total of $66. On the other hand, turning over each of the dozen cards in the stock costs you $60, so your net total will only be $6. Sure, you might get lucky and have the first card you flip from the stock start a run that clears the board, but it probably won't. You might not even have the right cards in the stock to clear off the last two peaks at all, which could end up costing you as much as $80 or $90. Be ready to quit while you're ahead… or even behind just a little.

Strategy. Although winning at TriPeaks is partly a matter of luck, you can improve your chances by following a few simple rules:

- Don't go so fast that you miss an opportunity. Remember, you can't undo a move. Once a card is covered up on the discard pile, it's gone forever.

- Always remove the card that exposes the most new cards.

- Try to set up large runs, even if it means you sometimes skip one or two small runs.

■ Keep as many cards exposed as you can.

■ If a run can go in more than one direction, choose the one that ultimately gives you the longest run. If two possible runs are the same length, take the run that exposes the most new cards.

■ Don't try to clear all three peaks every time—be ready to quit if that looks like a good idea.

CHAPTER 26

WordZap

he last (but by no means least) game in Entertainment Pack Three is WordZap, written by Michael Crick. WordZap bills itself as an "addictionary" game. This exciting game lets you match your vocabulary against the computer or a human opponent.

Michael Crick, the author of WordZap, saw a demonstration of Taipei and was inspired to create a word game that used tiles. This game, known as WordHai, was first published on the Commodore Amiga. When a version for the Nintendo Game Boy was planned, WordHai evolved to become WordZap, with one- and two-player capabilities.

Shortly thereafter, Charles Fitzgerald, the product manager for the Microsoft Entertainment Packs, asked Michael Crick if he had any games that ran under Windows. Crick, who used to teach part of the Advanced Windows Course at Microsoft University, quickly created a Windows game, and the rest, as they say, is history.

Object of the Game

The object of WordZap is to use the available letters to make seven three-, four-, or five-letter words before the computer or your opponent does. Your ability to win is a measure of your vocabulary and your speed at coming up with words.

Opening window
for EasyZap

Game Window

The WordZap window has the letter tiles on the left of the window and a word tray with space for seven words, each with a maximum length of five letters, on the right side. Empty spaces in the word tray are gray. The number of tiles you see on the left side of the screen depends on whether you're playing EasyZap (the default version of the game, shown here) or WordZap (which has fifteen letter tiles instead of eight). WordZap starts with the EasyZap version, and so should you, while you're learning.

If the Scoring option is on, you can see how many games your opponent has won compared to the number you've won, just beneath the letter tiles in the game window.

Play!

Starting the game. Start WordZap by double-clicking the WordZap icon in the Entertainment Pack Three group window. WordZap opens to a title screen. To start the game, choose New Game from the Game menu or press F2.

The word tray appears with eight letter tiles next to it, face down so you can't see the letters. Click the Ready button to start the game. As soon as you click the Ready

Easy Zap window showing several words in the word tray and the computer indicator going up, too

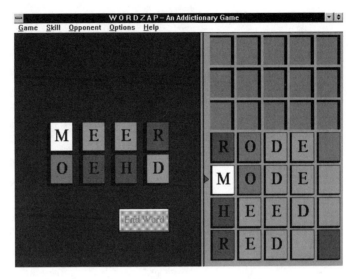

button, the computer turns over the tiles and starts looking for words, so don't just sit there—get going!

Moves. To spell a word, click on the letters in order. As you click on each letter, it zips to the next available space in the bottom row of the word tray. You can use each tile only once per word. For example, if you need two L's to spell PILL but you only have one L tile, you're out of luck.

Words must be at least three letters long to be acceptable. If you make a three- or four-letter word, you have to click the End Word button to tell the computer that you're ready to go on to the next word. When you place the fifth character in a five-letter word, WordZap knows that you're done and automatically goes to the next word.

If you spell a word that the computer doesn't know, a message such as, "Curious word," followed by the word in question, appears at the top of the game window. If you make a mistake spelling (by grabbing the wrong tile, for example), you can pull the last letter off of the word tray by right-clicking anywhere on the window or by pressing Backspace. If you want to remove the last few letters, click on the letter farthest to the left in the word; the computer removes that letter and all the others to the right of it. For instance, if you spell THONE when you meant to spell THINK, click on the O to remove the last three letters fast. To remove the entire word at once, click on the first letter in the word.

As you spell words, the computer compares them with the words on its own list. If at any time both of you have the same word, the word is "zapped" and removed from both lists of words. You can't use that word again this game. In other words, to win you need to be able to think up more words faster than the computer *and* you need to think of words the computer hasn't thought of. This can be a real challenge at the higher skill levels.

When you make a word, any blank spaces at the end of the word are colored. You can tell how well the computer is doing because the gray spaces in your word tray turn slate gray and the indicator arrow on the side of the tray moves up. If you zap the computer, the indicator goes down accordingly. The game continues until you or the computer gets seven words in your tray.

What's in WordZap's dictionary?

The dictionary has most three-, four-, and five-letter words found in U.S. dictionaries. Michael Crick's wife, Barbara, and her sister, Eva, collected and classified over 10,000 three-, four-, and five-letter words for WordZap. Some secondary spellings of words, such as "grey," were not included ("gray" being the preferred spelling).

When Nintendo released WordZap, they removed about two dozen words that they deemed unacceptable, including the words "sex" and "god." This means that if you try to spell "sex" or "god" during a game, the computer may respond with an amusing message such as "Unfamiliar with sex" and "I do not know the word 'GOD'." Interestingly enough, Microsoft also removed about two dozen words from WordZap's dictionary as being unacceptable, but only one word ("jap") was on both lists.

WordZap window,
showing different layout

WordZap EasyZap, the default game, gives you eight letters to work with in any order. WordZap gives you fifteen letters. After you choose the first letter, you can only use letters that touch the empty space left by the first letter on at least one of its four sides (diagonals don't count). For example, in this figure, you can spell PLEA but you can't spell PAGE because the A is at a diagonal to the P and isn't free. Except for this restriction and the additional number of tiles, the two games are played exactly the same way.

Options. To see how many games your opponent's won, compared to how many you've won, set the Scoring option in the Options menu to on. (There's a checkmark on the menu next to any option that's active.)

Choosing the Plurals option from the Options menu lets you use plural forms of words (such as TUBS) as well as third-person singular forms of words (such as TANS or GETS). Turning plurals on also lets you use more complex plurals such as "ova" and "zoa" (the plurals of "ovum" and "zoon"). If you really like to make longer words, go ahead and use this option, but if you're interested in winning, leave it off. Creating plurals usually just takes extra time.

If your monitor can handle 256 colors, you can choose Deluxe Set from the Options menu. This lets you use a more expensive-looking game. The rules and play are identical, but the deluxe set's wood-grain finish adds a certain swank.

Skill levels. You can tell the computer how big a vocabulary it can use by choosing Easier, Standard, or Hardest under Vocabulary Level on the Skill menu. Standard is just that. Easier is the vocabulary of an average twelve-year-old (which you may find shockingly limited), and Hardest is for those who like to curl up with a good dictionary in front of a roaring fire.

Although you may have told the computer to use only simple words, you are under no such restriction. Any word you enter is checked against the computer's dictionary for validity. Words such as "vug," "aver," "ell," "wen," and "coll" are all acceptable (look 'em up yourself if you don't know.) The computer won't recognize proper names, most slang, abbreviations, or ethnically offensive words.

From the keyboard

WordZap is a game designed largely for the mouse, but there are some keyboard shortcuts worth knowing about.

The Esc key not only does what it's supposed to do (blanks the screen instantly when the boss walks by), it pauses any game in progress so the computer can't cheat. Get Help by pressing F1, start a new game by pressing F2, and pause the game by pressing F3. Like Stones and several other games, when you pause the game, a cover comes down over the game window so you can't examine the board while you're paused. The Backspace key removes the last letter from a word, just like clicking on it in the word tray.

If you're using the Alt key and standard Windows-style keyboard shortcuts to get to the menus, watch out for Alt-O. Alt-O chooses first the Opponent menu and then the Options menu.

Handicaps. You can set the handicap anywhere from 36 to 15 by choosing Handicap from the Skill menu and moving the indicator along the bar to the desired level. The computer matches your handicap. The lower the number, the harder it is to beat the computer. If you want to play against the computer at a skill level less than 15 (that is, *mano a mano*), you're going to have to earn it. The computer won't let you set the skill level lower than 15; you have to beat the computer often enough that you work your way up the ranks. The computer remembers the handicap from session to session, so you don't have to start all over to work your way up to handicap 12. On the other hand, if you're playing WordZap on someone else's computer, you may want to check the handicap before you begin so you don't get whipsawed by the computer.

Handicap dialog box

When Auto-Handicap on the Options menu is on, the computer adjusts the handicap to reflect how well you're playing. As you win more games, the handicap (which is initially set at 30) goes down—and the computer gets faster and harder to beat. Bear in mind that if you lose games, the computer may adjust the handicap appropriately to take your (ahem) poorer playing into account.

As you progress up the ranks, you work your way up from being a "Nothing" to a "Word Wimp" to a "Word Nerd" to a "Word Hero" to a "Word Ace" to a "Word Maestro" (at level 15). Your rank changes every five levels. What's beyond level 15? You have to see for yourself, although getting to the final skill level (level 0) earns you the rank of "Golden" (and a resounding cheer from a crowd of awe-struck WordZap enthusiasts).

One thing you should know about handicaps: when playing another person, the computer compares the handicaps of the two players and may give the weaker player an advantage of one, two, or three words. If you see a message that says "Opponent's advantage increased to 1," it means that your opponent only has to make six words to win.

Playing WordZap with two people. WordZap was originally a two-player game, and many people think that it's best when played that way. To play WordZap against a real human opponent instead of the computer, connect your computer with your opponent's via the serial ports. You need a null modem cable to do this. (A null-modem cable has the wires to two of the pins switched. If you don't know what they are, ask your computer dealer to supply a ready-made cable. Null-modem cables cost somewhere around $10.) The null-modem cable plugs into a serial port on each of the two computers.

When you have the cable plugged in, choose Setup Communications from the Opponent menu. In the dialog box that appears, click on the port to which the cable is attached on that computer. For example, if you have the cable attached to COM2, click Com 2 in the box. Repeat this process on the other computer. When both computers are set up, click Connect in the dialog box to establish communications between the two computers. If the connection doesn't work, it might be because you chose the wrong serial ports on one or both computers. Keep trying. Once the settings are correct, click on Save Settings so WordZap remembers the settings next time you play.

Now when you go to the Opponent menu, both the Computer and the Human options are available. To play against another person, choose Human from the Opponent menu. The computers will establish communications and you can play against someone sitting next to you, down the hall, or even in another part of town. (To play against a remote Opponent, you have to know how to establish a modem link manually and then switch control over to the computer with a voice-data switch.) You can also connect (with a null-modem cable) the Microsoft Entertainment Pack version of WordZap to an Amiga running WordHai.

Once you have the communications link set up, you'll find that playing against a human opponent is virtually identical to playing against the computer.

Sending messages. One of the biggest advantages of playing against a human opponent is that you can now send rude messages about your adversary's playing ability, choice of words, ancestry, and personal habits, thanks to WordZap's message feature. When you type something on the keyboard, a dialog box appears automatically that accepts up to thirty-three characters. Press Enter or click OK to send the message to your opponent. The message you send appears on your opponent's game window, above the tiles. Depending on the content, your opponent may or may not send a gracious reply. A well-placed message at the right time may also strategically interrupt your opponent's thoughts. Consider the possibilities.

You can also send messages to the computer when you're playing by yourself. The computer even responds, although probably not as colorfully as a human opponent might. The computer has a number of stock answers for its comebacks.

Endgame. Both EasyZap and WordZap end when one player or another makes seven words on their tray. However, you can't always make seven words out of a combination of eight or fifteen letters, or you and the computer may zap each other back and forth until there aren't seven words left to make. If neither player has made a valid word for the last 25 seconds, a countdown begins. When the countdown reaches 10, the computer starts counting down on the screen. If the computer finishes its countdown, the player with the most words win. If the players have the same number of words, the player with the most letters wins. If the players have the same number of letters, it's a tie.

Scoring and Winning

Scoring is pretty much a win/lose thing in WordZap. You can keep track of how many games you've won against the computer by choosing Scoring on the Options menu. With Scoring turned on, the computer displays the number of games each player has won. Choose Reset on the Game menu to set the score back to 0:0. (If you're playing against a human rather than the computer, resetting your scores only affects the display of your own score. Your opponent's score is unchanged.)

Tips, Traps, and Sneaky Tricks

The faster you can get seven words out, the easier it is to win. Go for all the three-letter words you can find first, then shoot for the four- and five-letter words. Since it takes time to move the mouse around, look to see if one grouping of the tiles is richer in words than the rest and stay there as much as possible.

Learn to use mouse tricks to improve your speed. For example, you can remove a letter from the word tray by picking Back Up from the game menu or pressing Backspace, but both methods are relatively slow. The absolutely quickest way to pull a letter back is just to right-click anywhere on the game window. Similarly, you can pick End Word from the Game menu or move the pointer down and click on the End Word button when you make a word that's less than five letters long, but both of these cost you valuable time. The quickest way to tell WordZap that a word is finished is to double-click on the last letter you pick. WordZap places the letter in the tray and automatically ends the word.

The computer has no system for finding words in the letters—it just crunches through the dictionary (suitably scrambled) to find out what words it can make. The computer can't see words that are related or that have only one letter difference. You can use this to your advantage. Say you have the letters, L, A, N, E, P, C, D, and M. You could quickly win with LANE, PANE, CANE, DANE, PAN, CAN, and MAN by making that one-letter-difference association that the computer doesn't see.

Learning your opponent's strategy. Win or lose, you can see what your opponent's words were by clicking in the word tray when game is over. Even if you only played against the computer, it's a good idea to take a look—you may learn a few new words in the process.

If you're playing against a human being and they're close to winning, try to guess what words they have so you can zap them. This may be distracting enough to them that you can sail on to victory. The computer finds words more or less at random, so this trick won't work against the box.

If you've clearly beaten your opponent on points, the clock is counting down, and you see one more word you could make, don't bother. You don't get anything extra for the number of words you have on your tray; let the clock run out and take the win the easy way. If you enter another word, the clock restarts and your opponent has more time to get a flash of insight and beat you. In case your opponent comes up with something at the last second, though, you can spell that word you just saw and then be ready to click on the "End Word" button ... but only just in case.

Don't think out loud if you're playing someone else and they're near enough to hear you. On the other hand, if you're playing the computer, feel free to say anything you like to it.

You can remove the indicator on the side of the word tray that tells you how many words your opponent has. Open the ENTPACK.INI file in the Notepad or some other editor and add a line to the WordZap section that says "Marker=0." The marker won't appear when you play. You can still see the tiles on the word tray change color when your opponent is ahead of you, but without the indicator showing you won't know how much of a lead you have on your opponent. This adds excitement to the game, and may change some of your strategies.

While you're hacking about in ENTPACK.INI, you might also want to tweak the Handicap and Best indicators. Handicap is the current handicap, and Best is where the red line on the Handicap dialog box appears. You can set Handicap=0 if you want a brief but pungent full force encounter with the computer (you won't last). Changing Best lets you adjust the red line to your own pain threshold.

WordZap is available for the Nintendo Game Boy as WordHai. It may also be available soon for regular Nintendo systems as a one-player game. Check with your Nintendo game dealer for more information.